Irish Cures, Mystic Charms, and Superstitions

Lady Wilde

Illustrated by Marlene Ekman

 Sterling Publishing Co., Inc.   New York

Library of Congress Cataloging-in-Publication Data

Wilde, Lady, 1826–1896.
    Irish cures, mystic charms, & superstitions/Lady Wilde ;
illustrated by Marlene Ekman.
        p.   cm.
    "The material in this book has been compiled from Ancient legends,
mystic charms, and superstitions of Ireland and Ancient cures,
charms, and usages of Ireland, both by Lady Wilde, compiled by
Sheila Anne Barry"—CIP t.p.verso.
    Includes index.
    ISBN 0-8069-8200-4
    1. Folklore—Ireland. 2. Legends—Ireland. 3. Ireland—Social
life and customs. I. Barry, Sheila Anne. II. Wilde, Lady,
1826–1896. Ancient legends, mystic charms, and superstitions of
Ireland. III. Wilde, Lady, 1826–1896. Ancient cures, charms, and
usages of Ireland. IV. Title.
GR147.W52   1990
398'.09415—dc20   90-47066
                                                              CIP

The material in this book has been compiled
from *Ancient Legends, Mystic Charms & Superstitions
of Ireland* and *Ancient Cures, Charms, and
Usages of Ireland*, both by Lady Wilde.

Compiled by Sheila Anne Barry

10   9   8   7   6

Compilation and illustrations © 1991 by Sterling Publishing Co., Inc.
387 Park Avenue South, New York, N.Y. 10016
Distributed in Canada by Sterling Publishing
% Canadian Manda Group, P.O. Box 920, Station U
Toronto, Ontario, Canada M8Z 5P9
Distributed in Great Britain and Europe by Cassell PLC
Villiers House, 41/47 Strand, London WC2N 5JE, England
Distributed in Australia by Capricorn Ltd.
P.O. Box 665, Lane Cove, NSW 2066
Manufactured in the United States of America
All rights reserved
Sterling ISBN 0-8069-8200-4 Paper

CONTENTS

ANCIENT
CURES

ll nations and races from the earliest time have held the intuitive belief that mystic beings were always around them, influencing, though unseen, every action of life, and all the forces of nature. They felt the presence of a spirit in the winds, and the waves, and the swaying branches of the forest trees, and in the primal elements of all that exists. Fire was to them the sacred symbol of the divine essence, ever striking towards ascension; and water, ever seeking a level, was the emblem of the purification that should cover all daily life; while in the elemental earth they reverenced the power that produces all things, and where all that lives finds a grave, yet also a resurrection.

Thus to the primitive races of mankind the unseen world of mystery was a vital and vivid reality; the great over-soul of the visible, holding a mystic and psychic relation to humanity, and ruling it through the instrumentality of beings who had a strange power either for good or evil over human lives and actions.

We turn back the leaves of the national legends of all countries and peoples, and find stamped on the first page the words "God and Immortality." These two ideas are at the base of all the old-world thought and culture, and underlie all myths, rituals, and monuments, and all the antique usages and mystic lore of charms, incantations, and sacrificial observances.

The primal idea may be often degraded, debased, and obscured by the low instincts of savage man; yet, religious faith is the basis of all superstitions, and in all of them can be traced the ceaseless and instinctive effort of humanity to incarnate and make manifest this prescience within the soul of the *unseen* dominating the *seen*, with the desire, also, to master the forces of nature through the aid of these invisible spirits.

It is worthy of note, also, that the mythology of superstitions of a people are far more faithful guides as to the origin and affinity of races than language, which, through commerce and conquest, is perpetually changing, till the ancient idiom is at last crushed out and lost by the dominance of the stronger and conquering nation.

But the myths, superstitions, and legends (which are the expression of a people's faith), remain fixed and fast through successive generations, and finally become so inwoven with the daily life of the people that they form part of the national character and cannot be dissevered from it.

This is especially true of the Irish who, having been wholly separated from European thought and culture for countless centuries, by their language and insular position at the extreme limit of the known world, have remained unchanged in temperament and nature; still clinging to the old traditions with a fervour and faith that cannot be shaken by any amount of modern philosophic teaching. They are also, perhaps, indebted to Egypt for the wonderful knowledge of the power of herbs, which has always characterised the Irish, both amongst the adepts and the peasants.

The Irish Doctors

From the most ancient pagan times, the Irish doctors were renowned for their skill in the treatment of disease, and the professors of medicine held a high and influential position in the Druid order. They were allowed a distinguished place at the royal table, next to the nobles, and above the armourers, smiths, and workers in metals; they were also entitled to wear a special robe of honour when at the courts of the kings, and were always attended by a large staff of pupils, who assisted the master in the diagnosis and treatment of disease, and the preparations necessary for the curative potions.

The skill of the Irish physicians was based chiefly upon a profound knowledge of the healing nature and properties of herbs; and they were also well acquainted with the most deadly and concentrated poisons that can be found in the common field plants.

But, in addition to the aid given by science and observation, they also practised magic with great effect, knowing well how strongly charms, incantations, and fairy cures can act on the nerves and impress the mind of a patient. Consequently, their treatment of disease was of a medico-religious character, in which various magic ceremonials largely helped the curative process.

A few examples of these ancient cures and charms may be given to show their simple, half-religious character, so well calculated to impress a people like the Irish, of intense faith and a strong instinct for the mystic and the supernatural.

For ordinary disease there is nothing so good as the native poteen, for it is peculiarly adapted to the climate, and, as the people say, it keeps away ague and rheumatism, and the chill that strikes the heart; and if the gaugers would only let the private stills alone, not a bit of sickness would there be in the whole country round.

Take nine leaves of the male crowfoot, plucked on a Sunday night: bruise them on a stone that never was moved since the world began, and never can be moved. Mix with salt and spittle, and apply the plaster to the ear of the sick beast. Repeat this three times for a man, and twice for a horse.

For Ague

A few spiders tied up in a bag, and worn round the neck, will keep off fever and ague; but none, save the fairy doctor, must ever open the bag to look at the contents, or the charm would be broken.

For ague, a small living spider should be rolled up in a cobweb, then put into a lump of butter and eaten while the fit is on. Pills, also, may be made of the cobwebs in which the eggs remain, and taken daily for three days; after which time it would be dangerous to continue the treatment.

For Apoplexy

A spoonful of *aqua vitæ* sweetened with sugar, and a little grated bread added, that it may not annoy the brain or the liver, will preserve from lethargy and apoplexy and all cold diseases.

For Asthma

Let the patient drink of a potion made of dandelion (dent-de-lion—lion's tooth) or of ground-ivy, made and used in the same way, with prayer said over it before drinking.

For the Bite of a Mad Dog

Six ounces of rue, four ounces of garlic, two ounces of Venice treacle, and two ounces of pewter filings. Boil for two hours in a close vessel, in two quarts of ale, and give a spoonful fasting each morning till the cure is effected. The liquor is to be strained before use.

A charm which Columkill applied to a wound, brimful of poison, and it took away the venom:

"Arise, Cormac O'Clunan,
through Christ be thou healed.
By the hand of Christ be thou healed,
in blood, marrow, and bone,
and may the poison die in thee
as I sign the sign of the Cross."

This oration to be said over the person bitten, while butter is given him to eat. It may also be said over a cow or a horse, but never over a hog or dog.

The touch from the hand of a seventh son cures the bite of a mad dog. This is also an Italian superstition.

For the Blood

The juice of carrots boiled down is admirable for purifying the blood.

They say in Shark Island, that any man who rubs his tongue over a lizard's back will be given power to cure a burn by applying the tongue to the part affected.

It is believed in the South and West, that if a person is licked by the lizard called the "Mankeeper," he will never suffer from burns, and can even heal them in another by his touch; for a man one day having trod on a lizard, found that he had acquired this power by the contact.

In modern times a plaster of potatoes, scraped as for starch, is constantly applied for a burn, and gives great ease. Fried cabbage-leaves are also used by the people to deaden the pain; but a plant of house-leek affixed to the thatch of the roof should not be forgotten, as this preserves the inmates of the cabin from scalds, burns, and the danger of fire as long as it remains untouched.

Lay your right hand very softly over the burn, then repeat these words three times over unto yourself, giving a gentle blast each time from your mouth on the place burned:

> Old clod beneath the clay,
> Burn away, burn away.
> In the name of God be thou healed. AMEN.

After this the pain will cease, and a deep sleep will fall on the patient.

For Burns

There is a pretty secret to cure a burn without a scar:

> "Take sheep's suet and the rind of the elder-tree,
> boil both together, and the ointment will cure
> a burn without leaving a mark."

Blow upon the burn three times, repeating the words:

> Two angels sat upon a stone,
> One was Fire, the other Frost,
> Praise Father, Son, and Holy Ghost.

The ends of candles used at wakes are of great efficacy in curing burns.

For Colds

A porridge advised by Dianecht, chief physician of the Tuatha-de-Danans, has been handed down through the centuries for relief of ailments of the body, as cold, phlegm, throat cats, and the presence of living things in the body, as worms. It consists of hazel-buds, dandelion, chickweed, and wood sorrel, all boiled together with oatmeal. This porridge to be taken morning and evening, when the cold and the trouble will soon disappear. Also a poultice of yellow baywort tied round the throat is excellent as a cure for the throat cats.

For Contusions

Heat a great stone in the fire, and, when red-hot, throw it into water, and bathe the bruise with the liquid. Repeat this treatment twice a day, always first heating the stone, and the cure is certain in a few days.

For Convulsions

Clippings of the hair and nails of a child tied up in a linen cloth and placed under the cradle will cure convulsions.

For Cows

If a cow becomes restive, plunges about, or lies down with her nose to the ground, she is said to have the *peist*, or worm. To cure this, a long string is taken and twisted into a knot, like a coiled worm; and the curious knot seems so firmly knitted that it never could be untied. Yet there is a mode of drawing out the two ends, when the coil disappears and the string is quite free. This is done three times while the Paternoster is said over the animal, when the most beneficial result is sure to follow. This cure is called *snaidhenna-peista* (the worm's knot), and is of great antiquity.

If a cow suddenly falls sick, without any apparent cause, it is believed that she has swallowed an insect of the beetle kind, called *Derib*, which lives in ditches and stagnant pools. The remedy is to strike the animal three times across the loins, with a garment belonging to anyone of the name of Cassidy.

But if a cow is bewitched by the fairies and gives no milk, the owner must lead her three times round one of the ancient stone monuments near a holy well, casting an elf stone each time on the heap. And if this is not successful, then elf stones must be tied up in a cloth with a piece of money, and thrown into a vessel of water for the animal to drink. Some butter, also, may be added to propitiate the saint of the well, and after this the cow will surely recover.

For Cramp

An eel's skin tied round the knee alleviates pain.

For Deafness

Take the cowslip, roots, blossom, and leaves, clean them well, then bruise and press them in a linen cloth, add honey to the juice thus pressed out, put it in a bottle, and pour a few drops into the nostrils and ears of the patient, he lying on his back. Then, after some time, turn him on his face till the water pours out, carrying away whatever obstruction lay on the brain. This may be repeated for three days. Or fold up two eels in a cabbage-leaf, place them on the fire till they are soft, then press out the juice and drop it into the ears.

For Depression of Heart

When a person becomes low and depressed and careless about everything, as if all vital strength and energy had gone, he is said to have got a fairy blast. And blast-water must be poured over him by the hands of a fairy doctor while saying, "In the name of the saint with the sword, who has strength before God and stands at His right hand." Great care being taken that no portion of the water is profaned. Whatever is left after the operation, must be poured on the fire.

For Dropsy

Nettles gathered in a churchyard and boiled down for a drink have the power to cure dropsy.

For Dysentery

Woodbine and maiden-hair, pounded and boiled in new milk, with oatmeal, and taken three times a day, the leaves to be afterwards burned.

For Dyspepsia

Fix a small piece of candle on a penny piece, then lay the patient on his back and place the penny on the region of the stomach; light the candle, and over all place a well-dried tumbler, when the skin will be drawn up, as in cupping. This is called "the lifting of the evil from the body."

For Earache

Some wool taken from a black sheep, and worn constantly in the ear, is a sure remedy for earache.

For Epilepsy (Convulsions, the Falling Sickness)

Take nine pieces of young elder twig; run a thread of silk of three strands through the pieces, each piece being an inch long. Tie this round the patient's neck next the skin. Should the thread break and the amulet fall, it must be buried deep in the earth and another amulet made like the first, for if once it touches the ground the charm is lost.

Take nine pieces of a dead man's skull, grind them to powder, and then mix with a decoction of wall rue. Give the patient a spoonful of this mixture every morning fasting, till the whole potion is swallowed. None must be left, or the dead man would come to look for the pieces of his skull.

Another cure: A harrow-pin, a piece of money, and cuttings of the hair and nails of the patient are buried deep down in the earth, on the spot where he fell in the fit, and he is given a drink of holy water, in which nine hairs from the tail of a black cat have been steeped.

Take a hank of grey yarn, a lock of the patient's hair, some parings of his nails, and bury them deep in the earth, repeating, in Irish, as a burial service, "Let the great sickness lie there for ever. By the power of Mary and the soul of Paul, let the great sickness lie buried in the clay, and never more rise out of the ground. AMEN."

If the patient, on awaking from sleep, calls out the name of the person who uttered these words, his recovery is certain.

If a person crosses over the patient while he is in a fit, or stands between him and the fire, then the sickness will cleave to him and depart from the other that was afflicted.

Put salt and white snails into a vessel for three nights, add 7lb. woodbine leaves, and mix them to a paste; a poultice of this applied for nine days will cure.

Or, the heart of a crow, beaten up with his blood, and drank for nine days, will relieve the disease.

Or, a plaster made of mandragore and ground-ivy, boiled and laid upon the head. If the patient sleeps he will do well, and if not, he will not.

Or, a band of the fresh skin of a wolf worn round the body as a girdle, and as long as the patient wears it he will be free from the falling sickness.

Or, pour wine upon a pound of hemlock, fresh gathered, and let it be drank while the person is in the fit.

Or, three hairs of a milk-white greyhound to be tied up and worn on the neck as an amulet. This keeps the fit away.

The scribe who copied these receipts says of himself, "I am Conlan Mac Liagh son of the doctor, and in the Monastery of

Tuam I am this 14th day of the moon's age, and a thousand years, four hundred years, and nine years the age of the Lord."

For Erysipelas

Called by the Irish the "wild fire," is believed to originate from fairy malice; and blood must be spilled to cure the disease. The blood of a black cat is best, consequently few of these animals can be seen with an entire tail, for it is nipped off bit by bit to perform the cure.

For the Eyes

The most efficacious treatment for diseases of the eye is a pilgrimage to a holy well, for the blessed waters have a healing power for all ophthalmic ailments, and can even give sight to the blind.

Pearls upon the eye are said to be removed by an amber bead, the tenth upon the rosary, rubbed upon the eye; and the wise woman of the village will show the amber bead, with a white substance adhering, which she affirms is the pearl removed by the mystic attraction of the amber.

Also the shell of a living snail is pierced with a pin, and the fluid that exudes is used as healing for the eyes. This cure is called the "Snail Drop."

Severe counter-irritation upon the crown of the head has been long used by the wise women, and with wonderful success. The crown of the head is first shaved, and then a plaster is applied, made of coarse lint and white of egg spread upon a piece of tow.

This is left on till a blister rises, when the cure speedily follows.

This remedy of counter-irritation is, however, now well known and recognised by the medical profession, and largely used in ophthalmic surgery.

Fasting spittle is considered of great efficacy by the peasants for sore eyes, especially if mixed with clay taken from a holy well. This is made into a paste and applied to the eyes, and the people say "nothing beats the fasting spittle for blessedness."

The tail of a black cat rubbed on the eyes has marvellous curative properties, and the blood of a black cat is largely used in all mystic cures for disease.

A charge of great power, called "The Charge of the Artificer's Son," and from the Danes it was got; and these are the herbs: onions and dillisk, with ambrosia and garlic; and let the plants be broken and boiled upon beer; then add the gall of a hog's liver and a drop of wine or of doe's milk, and, when well strained, pour it into an amphora of brass, and apply the liquid to the eye, when the benefit is certain.

Another illustrious charge is made of white lily, valerian, and the leaves of the rowan tree. Also yarrow, and honey, and the gall of fish boiled together and strained, then applied to the eye, will carry off every description of blindness and clear the pains of the head.

For weak eyes: A decoction of the flowers of daisies boiled down is an excellent wash, to be used constantly.

For Fever

To cure fever, place the patient on the sandy shore when the tide is coming in, and the retreating waves will carry away the disease and leave him well.

"God save thee, Michael archangel! God save thee!"

"What aileth thee, O man?"

"A headache and a sickness and a weakness of the heart. O Michael, archangel, canst thou cure me, O angel of the Lord?"

"May three things cure thee, O man. May the shadow of Christ fall on thee! May the garment of Christ cover thee! May the breath of Christ breathe on thee! And when I come again thou wilt be healed."

These words are said over the patient while his arms are lifted in the form of a cross, and water is sprinkled on his head.

Take a ribbon and tie it tightly round the head of the sick person, saying: "In the name of Father, Son, and Holy Ghost, let the fever go from thy head, O man, and be thou healed."

For the Nine-Day Fever: Write the name of Jesus nine times on a slip of paper, then cut the paper into small bits, mix the pieces with some soft food, and make the patient swallow it. So will he be cured if he trusts in the Lord.

For Freckles

Anoint a freckled face with the blood of a bull, or of a hare, and it will put away the freckles and make the skin fair and clear. Also the distilled water of walnuts is good.

For a Headache

Measuring the head for nervous headache is much practised. The measuring doctor has certain days for practising his art, and receives or visits his patients on no other occasions. He first measures the head with a piece of tape above the ears and across the forehead, then from ear to ear over the crown of the head, then diagonally across the vertex. After this he uses strong compression with his hands, and declares that the head is "too open." And he mutters certain prayers and charms at the same time.

This process is repeated for three days, until at last the doctor asserts that the head is closing and has grown much smaller—in proof he shows his measurements; and the cure is completed when he pronounces the head to be "quite closed," on which the headache immediately vanishes, and the patient is never troubled by it again.

The corner of a sheet that has wrapped a corpse is a cure for headache if tied round the head.

For Hip Disease

Take three green stones, gathered from a running brook, between midnight and morning, while no word is said. In silence it must be done. Then uncover the limb and rub each stone several times closely downwards from the hip to the toe, saying in Irish—

> "Wear away, wear away,
> There you shall not stay,
> Cruel pain—away, away."

For Inflammation

Nine handfuls of mountain moss, dried on a pan to powder. Nine pinches of it, and nine pinches of the ashes from the hearth, to be mixed in whey, taken every Tuesday and Thursday.

For Influenza

For the *slaedan*, or influenza, some clay must be scraped off the threshold, made into a paste and applied as a plaster to the chest. But, to be effective, the clay must be taken from the very spot where a person first sets his foot on entering the house, when it is the custom to say, "God save all here," for these numerous blessings have given the clay a peculiar power to cure the chest and help the voice when it is affected. But the holy power is only for him who believes, for by his faith he will be made whole.

For Jaundice

The Homeopathic adepts amongst the Irish doctors always employ yellow medicines for the jaundice, as saffron, turmeric, sulphur, and even yellow soap. The Allopaths employ other remedies, especially the leaves of the barbary tree, which is held to be a specific, if brewed to a strong drink, and taken every morning, fasting, for nine days in succession.

An adept in the County Galway attracted great crowds to his dwelling recently by his wonderful cures for jaundice and other diseases. The remedy used was simply a dose of tartar emetic, administered freely for every form of ailment, and often the result was most satisfactory.

The fairy-doctors use the following cure:

Nine young shoots from the root of an ash tree that had been cut down. These are placed in a bottle, which is then buried in a secluded spot, the patient not being allowed to see it.

As long as the bottle remains in the ground, he is safe from the disease; but, should it be broken he will have a relapse and probably die from mental emotion, caused by fear of the result, before many days are over.

For the King's Evil (Scrofula)

There are certain wise men amongst the peasants who keep pieces of paper, transmitted from their fathers, which, they say, have been steeped in a king's blood. And if the paper is rubbed over the patient in the name of the Trinity, he will be cured.

A most effective cure of proved power is made of burdock roots, the common dock, bog-bean, and rose-noble boiled in water, of which the patient must drink three times a day.

Madness

There was a terrible cure employed in old times for insanity, which the people believed in with implicit faith. It consisted in burying the patient for three days and three nights in the earth. A pit was dug, three feet wide and six feet deep, in which the patient was placed, only the head being left uncovered; and during the time of the cure he was allowed no food, and no one was permitted to speak to him, or even to approach him. A harrow-pin was placed over his body, for the harrow-pin is supposed to have peculiar mystic attributes, and was always used in ancient sorceries, and then the unhappy patient was left alone. If he survived the living burial, he was generally taken out of the pit more dead than alive, perished with cold and hunger, and more mad than ever. Yet it was averred that sometimes the senses were actually restored by this inhuman treatment.

Madness is also cured by giving the person three substances not procured by human means, and not made by the hand of man.

These are honey, milk, and salt, and they are to be given him to drink before sunrise in a sea-shell. Madness and the falling sickness (convulsions, epilepsy) are both considered hereditary, and caused by demoniacal possession.

For the Measles

" 'The child has the measles,' said John the Baptist.
" 'The time is short till he is well,' said the Son of God.
" 'When?' said John the Baptist.
" 'Sunday morning, before sunrise,' said the Son of God."
   This is to be repeated three times, kneeling at a cross, for three mornings before sunrise, and the child will be cured by the Sunday following.

For the Memory

The whitest of frankincense beaten fine, and drunk in white wine, wonderfully assisteth the memory, and is profitable for the stomach also.

For the Liver Complaint

The leaves of plantain, wild sage, the shamrock and dock-leaf, with valerian and the flower of the daisy, are to be plucked by the person before sunrise, and fasting, on Mondays and Wednesdays, while Hail Mary is said, and the Paternoster; all these are to be boiled and strained, and the herbs afterwards to be carefully burned. A glassful of the liquor to be taken twice a day.

For Lumbago

Dog-fern roots and shamrocks should be cleaned and pounded

well, then mixed with butter—made on May morning—and holy salt, till a kind of paste is formed. This is rubbed all over the back, while the Lord's Prayer is said, and the Hail Mary; and the paste is by no means to be washed off, but left till the cure is perfected.

For the Mumps

Wrap the child in a blanket, take it to the pigsty, rub the child's head to the back of a pig, and the mumps will leave it and pass from the child to the animal.

Take nine black stones gathered before sunrise, and bring the patient with a rope around his neck to a holy well—not speaking all the while. Then cast in three stones in the name of God, three in the name of Christ, and three in the name of Mary. Repeat this process for three mornings and the disease will be cured.

Tie a halter around the child's neck, then lead him to a brook and bathe him, dipping him three times in the name of the Trinity.

For a Pain in the Side

"God save you, my three brothers, God save you! And how far have ye to go, my three brothers?"

"To the Mount of Olivet, to bring back gold for a cup to hold the tears of Christ."

"Go, then. Gather the gold; and may the tears of Christ fall on it, and thou wilt be cured, both body and soul."

These words must be said while a drink is given to the patient.

For Pains

"I kill the evil; I kill the worm in the flesh, the worm in the grass. I put a venomous charm in the murderous pain. The charm that was set by Peter and Paul; the charm that kills the worm in the flesh, in the tooth, in the body."

This oration to be said three times, while the patient is rubbed with butter on the place of the pain.

A happy mild charm, a charm which Christ discovered. The charm that kills the worm in the flesh.

"May Peter take, may Paul take, may Michael take, the pain away, the cruel pain that kills the back and the life, and darkens the eyes."

This oration written, and tied to a hare's foot, is always to be worn by the person afflicted, hung round the neck.

Rub the part affected with flax and tow, heated in the fire, repeating in Irish—

"In the name of a rough man and a mild woman, and of the Lamb of God, be healed from your pains and your sins. So be it. AMEN."

This custom refers to the tradition that one day the Lord Christ, being weary, asked leave to rest in a house, but was refused by the master of the house, a rough, rude man. Then the wife, being a mild woman, had pity on the wayfarer, and brought Him in to rest, and gave Him a cup of water to drink, and spake kindly to Him. After which the man was suddenly taken with severe pains, and seemed like to die in his agony.

On this Christ called for some flax and tow, and breathing on it, placed it on the part affected, by which means the man was quite healed. And then the Lord Christ went His way, but not before the man had humbly asked pardon for his rudeness to a stranger.

The tradition of this cure has remained ever since, and a hot plaster of flax and tow is used by the peasantry invariably for all sudden pains, and found to be most efficacious as a cure.

For the Red Rash

The red rash is cured by applying unsalted butter to the part affected, while the Ave Maria is said. Also the blood of a hare is very efficacious if applied to the skin with a red rag, and the rag afterwards buried.

For Rheumatism

The bone of the haddock that lies under the mark of Christ's fingers is always to be carried in the pocket. This bone has many other virtues, and always works good to the owner; but it must not be exhibited, and it should never be lent, or touched except by the owner.

Rheumatism was chiefly cured by stroking, and all remedies that acted on the imagination, such as lying in a saint's bed, mesmeric charms, and incantations, were deemed most effectual. Latin words were used as charms, sewn up in a bag and carried in the pocket, tied round the hind legs of a hare. An eel-skin had great virtue placed on the chest, or tied round the knee. Forge water had many virtues and could allay rheumatic pains; also potato water, used hot, with the froth on.

For Rickets

A blacksmith, whose fathers have been smiths for three generations, must carry the child in his apron three times round the anvil for seven days in succession, repeating the Paternoster each time. But no money must be accepted for the cure.

For St. Anthony's Fire (an inflammatory or gangrenous skin condition)

"The fire of earth is hot, and the fire of hell is hotter; but the love of Mary is above all. Who will quench the fire? Who will heal the sick? May the fire of God consume the Evil One! AMEN."

For a Sprain

In the Western Isles the following charm is used for a sprain.

A strand of black wool is wound round and round the ankle, while the operator recites in a low voice:

"The Lord rade and the foal slade,
He lighted and He righted;
Set joint to joint and bone to bone,
And sinew unto sinew.
In the name of God and the Saints,
Of Mary and her Son,
Let this man be healed. AMEN."

A similar charm was used in Germany in the tenth century, according to Jacob Grimm.

A young girl, under fourteen years of age, spins a thread dry, that is, without using saliva; then she ties it round the leg or the arm afflicted, and when the cure is completed the thread miraculously disappears. Chickweed is also used as a poultice. Galen notices the virtue of this herb, and extols its use to remove stiffness or swellings.

For a Stitch in the Side

Rub the part affected with unsalted butter, and make the sign of the cross seven times over the place.

For Stomach Disorders

A bunch of mint tied round the wrist is a sure remedy.

For a Stye on the Eyelid

Point a gooseberry thorn at it nine times, saying, "Away, away, away!" and the stye will vanish presently and disappear.

The tail of a black cat, if rubbed over the eye, will effect a speedy cure. It is good, also, to point nine thorns in succession at the eye, without touching it, throwing away each one after use over the left shoulder.

For Toothache

Go to a graveyard; kneel upon any grave; say three paters and three aves for the soul of the dead lying beneath. Then take a handful of grass from the grave, chew it well, casting forth each bite without swallowing any portion. After this process the sufferer, were he to live a hundred years, will never have toothache any more.

The patient must vow a vow to God, the Virgin, and the new moon, never to comb his hair on a Friday, in remembrance of relief should he be cured; and whenever or wherever he first sees the moon he must fall on his knees and say five prayers in gratitude for the cure, even if crossing a river at the time.

Carry in your pocket the two jaw-bones of a haddock; for ever since the miracle of the loaves and fishes these bones are an infallible remedy against toothache, and the older they are the better, as nearer the time of the miracle.

To avoid toothache never shave on a Sunday.

The tooth of a dead horse or the hand of a dead man rubbed over the jaw, will also be found effective to ease the pain of an ailing tooth.

To Remove Warts

On meeting a funeral, take some of the clay from under the feet of the men who bear the coffin and apply it to the wart, wishing strongly at the same time that it may disappear; and so it will be.

Tie up some pebbles in a bag with a piece of silver money, and throw it on the road; whoever finds the bag and keeps the money, to him the warts will go, and leave you for ever. Also, steal a piece of meat and apply it raw to the warts; then bury it in the ground, and as the meat decays the warts will disappear. But the charm is of no use unless the meat is stolen, and no one should see you either stealing or burying it.

For Water on the Brain

Cover the head well with wool, then place oil-skin over, and the water will be drawn up out of the head. When the wool is quite saturated the brain will be free and the child cured.

For Weakness

Drink of the water of a river forming the boundary of three properties for nine Sunday mornings, before sunrise, fasting, and before any one has crossed the stream. In silence it must be done, and without speaking to any one; but afterwards repeat nine *Aves* and the *Credo*.

A black spider, laid as a sandwich between two slices of bread-and-butter, and eaten—one every morning—will be found a great strengthener of the body.

For Whooping Cough

For whooping cough, a lock of hair, cut from the head of a person who never saw his father, is to be tied up in a piece of red cloth and worn round the neck.

Take a mug of water from a running stream, against the current; give the child a drink, then throw the rest away with the current; repeat this for three mornings before sunrise, and the cure will be perfected.

Put a live trout into the child's mouth, fasting. Then put it back alive into the stream. If a trout cannot be had, a frog may be tried.

MYSTIC CHARMS, SPELLS, AND INCANTATIONS

he ancient Druidic charms and invocations continued to hold their power over the people, who believed in them with undoubting faith. No doubt, in pagan times, the invocations were made in the names of Baal and Ashtaroth, and by the power of the sun, the moon, and the winds; but the Christian converts, while still retaining the form of the ancient charms, substituted the names of the Trinity and the words of the Christian Ritual as still more powerful in effecting cures. And in this mode they are used to the present day amongst the peasants, who consider them as talismans of magic power when said over the sick; and no amount of argument would shake their faith in these mystic formulas which have come down to them through centuries of tradition; nor would any one venture to laugh at them, or an evil fate would certainly fall on the scorner. For, above all things, fervent faith is necessary while the mystic words are uttered, or the charm will not work for good.

For Safety

Pluck ten blades of yarrow, keep nine, and cast the tenth away for tithe to the spirits. Put the nine in your stocking, under the heel of the right foot, when going a journey, and the Evil One will have no power over you.

A Blessing

"O aged old woman of the grey locks, may eight hundred blessings twelve times over be on thee! Mayest thou be free from desolation, O woman of the aged frame! And may many tears fall on thy grave."

How To Go Invisible

Get a raven's heart, split it open with a black-hafted knife; make three cuts and place a black bean in each cut. Then plant it, and when the beans sprout put one in your mouth and say—

> "By virtue of Satan's heart,
>   And by strength of my great art,
>   I desire to be invisible."

And so it will be as long as the bean is kept in the mouth.

How To Have Money Always

Kill a black cock, and go to the meeting of three cross-roads where a murderer is buried. Throw the dead bird over your left shoulder then and there, after nightfall, in the name of the devil, holding a piece of money in your hand all the while. And ever after, no matter what you spend, you will always find the same piece of money undiminished in your pocket.

For Barrenness

The seed of docks tied to the left arm of a woman will prevent her from being barren.

For Tasks

To Tame a Horse

Whisper the Creed in his right ear on a Friday, and again in his left ear on a Wednesday. Do this weekly till he is tamed; for so he will be.

To Attract Bees

Gather foxglove, raspberry leaves, wild marjoram, mint, camomile, and valerian; mix them with butter made on May Day, and let the herbs also be gathered on May Day. Boil them all together with honey; then rub the vessel into which the bees should gather, both inside and out, with the mixture; place it in the middle of a tree, and the bees will soon come. Foxglove or "fairy fingers" is called "the great herb" from its wondrous properties.

To Extract a Thorn

"The briar that spreads, the thorn that grows, the sharp spike that pierced the brow of Christ, give you power to draw this thorn from the flesh, or let it perish inside; in the name of the Trinity. AMEN."

To Find Stolen Goods

Place two keys on a sieve, in the form of a cross. Two men hold the sieve, while a third makes the sign of the cross on the forehead of the suspected party, and calls out his name loudly, three times over. If innocent, the keys remain stationary; but if guilty, the keys revolve slowly round the sieve, and then there is no doubt as to who is the thief.

For Healing

For a Wound

Close the wound tightly with the two fingers, and repeat these words slowly:

"In the name of the Father, Son, and Holy Mary. The wound was red, the cut was deep, and the flesh was sore; but there will be no more blood, and no more pain, till the blessed Virgin Mary bears a child again."

For a Wound that Bleeds

"A child was baptized in the river Jordan; and the water was dark and muddy, but the child was pure and beautiful." Say these words over the wound, placing the finger on the spot where the blood flows, adding: "In the name of God and of the Lord Christ, Let the blood be staunched." And if the patient have faith, so it will be.

For the Staunching of Blood

"There came a man from Bethlehem to be baptized in the river Jordan; but the water was so muddy that it stopped flowing. So let the blood! So let the blood! Let it stop flowing in the name of Jesus, and by the power of Christ!" This is said in a loud voice over the patient, while a scarlet worsted is tied tightly round the wrists and round the throat, to stop the course of the blood.

The spider's web is also an excellent styptic, and is still in use amongst all classes for the staunching of blood, or any abrasion of the skin.

A Very Ancient Charm against Wounds or Poisons

"The poison of a serpent, the venom of the dog, the sharpness of the spear, doth not well in man. The blood of one dog, the blood of many dogs, the blood of the hound of Fliethas—these I invoke. It is not a wart to which my spittle is applied. I strike disease; I strike wounds. I strike the disease of the dog that bites, of the thorn that wounds, of the iron that strikes. I invoke the three daughters of Fliethas against the serpent. Benediction on this body to be healed; benediction on the spittle; benediction on him who casts out the disease. In the name of God. AMEN."

For Protection

Against the Plague

"O Star of Heaven, beloved of the Lord, drive away the foul constellation that has slain the people with the wound of dreadful death. O Star of the sea, save us from the poison-breath that kills, from the enemy that slays in the night. AMEN."

Against Enemies

"Three things are of the Evil One—

> An evil eye;
> An evil tongue;
> An evil mind.

"Three things are of God; and these three are what Mary told to her Son, for she heard them in heaven—

> The merciful word;
> The singing word;
> And the good word.

"May the power of these three holy things be on all the men and women of Erin for evermore."

Against Accidents, Fire, Tempests, Water, Knife, or Lance

"Jesus, Saviour of men. In Jesus trust, and in Mary trust truly for all grace.

"This is the measure of the wounds of Christ upon the Cross, which was brought to Constantinople to the Emperor as a most precious relic, so that no evil enemy might have power over him. And whoever reads it, or hears it, cannot be hurt by fire or tempest, or the knife, or the lance; neither can the devil have power over him, nor will he die an untimely death, but safety from all dangers will be his to the end."

Against Drowning

"May Christ and His saints stand between you and harm.

> Mary and her Son.
> St. Patrick with his staff.
> Martin with his mantle.
> Bridget with her veil.
> Michael with his shield.

And God over all with His strong right hand."

In Time of Battle

"O Mary, who had the victory over all women, give me victory now over my enemies, that they may fall to the ground, as wheat when it is mown."

Against Ill-Luck

The most powerful charm against ill-luck is a horse-shoe made red-hot, then tied up at the entrance door, and never after touched or taken down.

For Undoing Fairy Stroke and Witchcraft

Against the Fairy Stroke

There is a very ancient and potent charm which may be tried with great effect in case of a suspected fairy-stroke.

Place three rows of salt on a table in three lines, three equal measures to each row. The person performing the spell then encloses the rows of salt with his arm, leaning his head down over them, while he repeats the Lord's Prayer three times over each row—that is, nine times in all. Then he takes the hand of the one who has been fairy-struck, and says over it, "By the power of the Father, and of the Son, and of the Holy Spirit, let this disease depart, and the spell of the evil spirits be broken! I adjure, I command you to leave this man [naming him]. In the name of God I pray; in the name of Christ I adjure; in the name of the Spirit of God I command and compel you to go back and leave this man free! AMEN! AMEN! AMEN!"

To Cure a Fairy-Stricken Child

Make a good fire, throw into it a handful or more of certain herbs ordered by the fairy-women; wait till a great smoke rises, then carry the child three times round the fire, reciting an incantation against evil, and sprinkling holy water all around. But during the process no door must be opened, or the fairies would come in to see what you were doing. Continue reciting the incantation till the child sneezes three times; then you may know that the fairy spell is broken, and the child has been redeemed from fairy thraldom for evermore. It is good, however, in addition, to tie a small bag round his neck, with three rounds of red ribbon or thread, containing a nail from the shoe of an ass and some hair of a black cat, and let this be worn for a year and a day.

A black cat without any white spot has great power either for or against witchcraft, and the hair must be taken from a cat of this description, for the demons fear it. Also, about midnight, give the child a drink mixed with the blood of a crowing hen; then he will be safe from fairy, or demon, or the evil of witchcraft.

To Cure an Animal Who Has Been Fairy-struck

Pass a red-hot turf three times over and under the body of an animal supposed to be fairy-struck, singeing the hair along the back. This drives off the fairies.

Against Alectromantia

Should a person be bewitched by an evil neighbour, he must take two black cocks, lay a charm over the head of one and let it loose; but the other must be boiled down, feathers and all, and eaten. Then the malice of the neighbour will have no effect on him or his.

Ancient Egypt and Greece had likewise superstitions on the subject of sacrificing a cock. Even the last words of Socrates had reference to this subject. It is remarkable also that in the Christian legend it was a cock that testified indignantly by his crowing against Peter's treachery and cowardice, and aroused in him the remorse that was evidenced by his tears.

Against the Evil Eye

This is a charm Mary gave to St. Bridget, and she wrote it down, and hid it in the hair of her head, without deceit—

"If a fairy, or a man, or a woman hath overlooked thee, there are three greater in heaven who will cast all evil from thee into the great and terrible sea. Pray to them, and to the seven angels of God, and they will watch over thee. AMEN."

To avert the evil eye from child or beast, it is necessary to spit upon it on entering a cabin; and if a stranger looks fixedly and admiringly on a child, he is at once requested to spit upon it; this saving process being perhaps unknown to him; or if he should not understand Irish, and omit the rite that preserves from evil, then the old mother will rise up from her seat by the fire and perform the ceremony herself, that so good luck may not depart from the house.

Vervain and the mountain ash are the best preservatives for cattle against witchcraft. Some should be tied round the cow's horns and her tail. Then no fairy or witch can do harm while the herbs of power are on her.

For Love

Philters, love powders, and charms to procure affection were frequently used in Ireland, and the belief in them existed from the most ancient times.

The bardic legends have frequent allusions to love charms; but the most awful of all is the dead strip. Girls have been known to go to a graveyard at night, exhume a corpse that had been nine days buried, and tear down a strip of the skin from head to foot; this they manage to tie round the leg or arm of the man they love while he sleeps, taking care to remove it before his awaking. And so long as the girl keeps this strip of skin in her possession, secretly hidden from all eyes, so long will she retain the man's love.

To Win Her Love

"O Christ, by your five wounds, by the nine orders of angels, if this woman is ordained for me, let me hold her hand now, and breathe her breath. O my love, I set a charm to the top of your head; to the sole of your foot; to each side of your breast, that you may not leave me nor forsake me. As a foal after the mare, as a child after the mother, may you follow and stay with me till death comes to part us asunder. AMEN."

A charm of most desperate love, to be written with a raven's quill in the blood of the ring finger of the left hand.

"By the power that Christ brought from heaven, mayest thou love me, woman! As the sun follows its course, mayest thou follow me. As light to the eye, as bread to the hungry, as joy to the heart, may thy presence be with me, O woman that I love, till death comes to part us asunder."

To Cause Love

Golden butter on a new-made dish, such as Mary set before Christ. This to be given in the presence of a mill, of a stream, and the presence of a tree; the lover saying softly—

"O woman, loved by me, mayest thou give me thy heart, thy soul and body. AMEN."

Ten leaves of the hemlock dried and powdered and mixed in food or drink will make the person you like to love you in return.

Also keep a sprig of mint in your hand till the herb grows moist and warm, then take hold of the hand of the woman you love, and she will follow you as long as the two hands close over the herb. No invocation is necessary; but silence must be kept between the two parties for ten minutes, to give the charm time to work with due efficacy.

If a potion is made up of herbs it must be paid for in silver; but charms and incantations are never paid for, or they would lose their power. A present, however, may be accepted as an offering of gratitude.

For Faithfulness

This is a charm I set for love; a woman's charm of love and desire; a charm of God that none can break—

"You for me, and I for thee and for none else; your face to mine, and your head turned away from all others."

This is to be repeated three times secretly, over a drink given to the one beloved.

Love Dreams

The girl who wishes to see her future husband must go out and gather certain herbs in the light of the full moon of the new year, repeating this charm—

> "Moon, moon, tell unto me
> When my true love I shall see?
> What fine clothes am I to wear?
> How many children shall I bear?
> For if my love comes not to me
> Dark and dismal my life will be."

Then the girl, cutting three pieces of clay from the sod with a black-hafted knife, carries them home, ties them up in the left stocking with the right garter, places the parcel under her pillow, and dreams a true dream of the man she is to marry and of all her future fate.

An Elixir of Potency

Two ounces of cochineal, one ounce of gentian root, two drachms of saffron, two drachms of snakeroot, two drachms of salt of wormwood, and the rind of ten oranges. The whole to be steeped in a quart of brandy, and kept for use.

To Cause Hatred Between Lovers

Take a handful of clay from a new-made grave, and shake it between them, saying:

"Hate ye one another! May ye be as hateful to each other as sin to Christ, as bread eaten without blessing is to God."

Malefic Charms

Not only are charms and incantations employed for curing disease, but they are also used to induce disease and death, in the form of maledictions and curses, and in the name of the Evil One.

A sheaf of corn is sometimes buried with a certain form of dedication to Satan, in the belief that as the corn rots in the ground, so will the person wither away who is under the curse.

Another form of malediction is to bury a lighted candle by night in a churchyard, with certain weird ceremonies. A young village girl, who had been treated badly by her lover, determined on revenge, and adopted this mode of curse upon him. He was a fine, healthy young fellow; but suddenly he began to pine and dwindle away, and then every one knew that the girl must have buried a candle against him. Great efforts were made to induce her to tell where it was buried, but she resisted all entreaty. At last, however, the candle was found, and the man had to eat it in order to neutralise the curse. Yet even this disagreeable remedy was of no avail, for the young man still continued to pine away, and in a short time he lay dead.

Maledictions

Epidemic diseases that will carry off an entire family can also be produced by the devil's magic, and smiths and old women are generally adepts in the black art. St. Patrick prayed to be delivered from smiths, women, and Druids; and even to the present time the smith is considered powerful in the working of charms, either for a blessing or a curse, and the peasants are cautious not to offend him.

The Lusmore, or Fairy-finger, is a deadly poison, and sometimes has been used in malice to produce convulsions in children.

In the case of a sudden fainting or swoon, the individual is supposed to be struck by a curse, and if he is unable to answer questions, he is tried with a grannoge, or hedgehog, and if it erects the spine it is a sure sign that the person is under the influence of the devil. Or the suspected person is wrapped in a woman's red cloak, with the hood over the head, and laid in a grave cut two feet deep. There he remains some hours covered with clay, all but the face, and if he becomes delirious and raves, then the people know that the devils are round him, and his death is considered certain.

The Dead Hand

To obtain the power and secrets of witchcraft, it is necessary to visit a churchyard at midnight, and cut off the hand of a recently buried corpse with your own hand. This is preserved by drying or smoking, and can then be used with great and fatal effect.

Stroking by the hand of a dead man can cure many diseases. It has also the power to bring butter to the churn, if the milk is stirred round nine times with it while a witch-prayer is recited. But many awful things must be done, and evil rites practised, before the witch-words can be learned and uttered.

OMENS AND
PROPHECIES

uguries and prophecies of coming fate may also be obtained from the flight of birds, the motion of the winds, from sneezing, dreams, lots, and the signs from a verse of the Psalter or Gospels. The peasantry attach great importance to the first verses of St. John's Gospel, and maintain that when the cock crows in the morning he is repeating these verses (from the 1st to the 14th), and if we understood the language of animals and birds, we could often hear them quoting these same verses.

A charm against sickness is an amulet worn round the neck, enclosing a piece of paper, on which is written the first three verses of St. John's Gospel.

Omens That Forbode Evil

To stick a penknife in the mast of a boat when sailing is most unlucky.

It is unlucky to meet a cat, a dog, or a woman, when going out first in the morning; but unlucky above all is it to meet a woman with red hair the first thing in the morning when going on a journey, for her presence brings ill-luck and certain evil.

To meet a man with red hair, or a woman with a red petticoat, the first thing in the morning.

To have a hare cross your path before sunrise.

To pass a churn and not give a helping hand.

To meet a funeral and not go back three steps with it.

It is unlucky to pass under a hempen rope; the person who does so will die a violent death, or is fated to commit an evil act in after life, so it is decreed.

To take away a lighted sod on May days or churning days; for fire is the most sacred of all things, and you take away the blessing from the house along with it.

It is unlucky and a bad omen to carry fire out of a house where any one is ill.

If a chair fall as a person rises, it is an unlucky omen.

If the ear itches and is red and hot, someone is speaking ill of you.

At Hallowtide (November 1) the air was filled with the presence of the dead, and everything around became a symbol or prophecy of fate. The name of a person called from the outside was a most dangerous omen; but if repeated three times, the result was fatal.

Birds also came as messengers of fate during Hallowtide, and their appearance was generally a prognostication of evil.

It is well to know that if a bird of ill omen should happen to come to the house, such as the raven or the water-wagtail, who is Satan's own emissary, the best way to turn aside the evil influence is to say at once: "Fire and water be on you, and in your mouth; and may the curse be on your head, O bird of evil, for evermore." And further, three candles must never be left lighted at once in the room.

It is unlucky to offer your left hand in salutation, for there is an old saying: "A curse with the left hand to those we hate, but the right hand to those we honour."

It is unlucky to accept a lock of hair, or a four-footed beast from a lover.

A hen that crows is very unlucky and should be killed; very often the hen is stoned, for it is believed that she is bewitched by the fairies.

If a man is ploughing, no one should cross the path of the horses.

It is unlucky to steal a plough, or take anything by stealth from a smith's forge.

When yawning make the sign of the cross instantly over the mouth, or the evil spirit will make a rush down and take up his abode within you.

Beware of a childless woman who looks fixedly at your child.

Never give away water before breakfast, nor milk while churning is going on.

Never give any salt or fire while churning is going on. To upset the salt is exceedingly unlucky and a bad omen; to avert evil gather up the salt and fling it over the right shoulder into the fire, with the left hand.

Do not put out a light while people are at supper, or there will be one less at the table before the year is out.

Never mend a rent in a dress while on, or evil and malicious reports will be spread about you.

Amongst fatal signs, the most fatal is to break a looking-glass, for then it is certain that someone in the house will die before the year is out. And there is no mode of averting the evil fate.

It is very unlucky to meet a weasel coming towards you in the early morning, and you should at once spit at him, for, if he spits at you first, a great danger will fall on you before the sun sets. Yet, you must never kill a weasel; it is fatal, and will bring sure destruction on yourself, for the whole family of the murdered weasel will take vengeance and cause something dreadful to happen to you within the year.

When changing your residence, it is unlucky to bring a cat with you, especially across a stream, and a red and white cat is particularly ominous and dangerous. If a black cat comes of her own accord to your house, keep her, she is a good spirit; but do not bring her, she must come freely, of her own good will.

Whoever kills a robin redbreast will never have good luck were they to live a thousand years.

A water wagtail near the house betokens bad news on its way.

If the first lamb of the season is born black, it foretells mourning garments for the family within the year.

It is unlucky to meet a magpie, a cat, or a lame woman when going a journey. Or for a cock to meet a person in the doorway and crow before him—then the journey should be put off.

If one magpie comes chattering to your door it is a sign of death; but if two prosperity will follow. For a magpie to come to the door and look at you is a sure death-sign, and nothing can avert the doom.

A flight of rooks over an army betokens defeat; if over a house, or over people when driving or walking, death will follow.

It is very unlucky to ask a man on his way to fish where he is going. And many would turn back, knowing that it was an evil spell.

When a swarm of bees suddenly quits the hive it is a sign that death is hovering near the house. But the evil may be averted by the powerful prayers and exorcism of the priest.

A crowing hen, a whistling girl, and a black cat, are considered most unlucky. Beware of them in a house.

If a hen crows on the roost it is a sign that the fairies have struck it, and the head of the hen must be immediately cut off and flung on the ground, or one of the family will sure die before the year is out.

Omens That Foretell Good Luck

The cricket is looked upon as a most lucky inmate of a house, and woe to the person who may happen to kill one; for all the other crickets will meet in general assembly and eat up the offender's clothes, as a just retribution for the loss of a friend and relation.

Never disturb the swallows, wherever they may build, and neither remove nor destroy their nests; for they are wise birds, and will mark your conduct either for punishment or favour.

If, by accident, you find the back tooth of a horse, carry it about with you as long as you live, and you will never want money; but it must be found by chance.

A purse made from a weasel's skin will never want for money; but the purse must be found, not given or made.

A coal of fire thrown after the fisherman brings him good fortune.

If the palm of the hand itches you will be getting money; if the elbow, you will be changing beds.

To see three magpies on the left hand when on a journey is unlucky; but two on the right hand is a good omen.

If you hear the cuckoo on your right hand you will have luck all the year after.

It is very lucky for a hen and her chickens to stray into your house. Also it is good to meet a white lamb in the early morning with the sunlight on its face.

To throw a slipper after a party-going journey is lucky. Also to breakfast by candle-light on Christmas morning.

Prophecies

Take a piece of bride-cake and pass it three times through a wedding-ring, then sleep on it, and you will see in a dream the face of your future spouse.

It is fatal at a marriage to tie a knot in a red handkerchief, and only an enemy would do it. To break the spell the handkerchief should be burned.

Those who marry in autumn will die in spring.

The fortunate possessor of the four-leaved shamrock will have luck in gambling, luck in racing, and witchcraft will have no power over him. But he must always carry it about his person, and never give it away, or even show it to another.

If any one is sick in the house, and the cock crows with his head to the fire, recovery may be expected; but if he crows with his head to the door, then death is certain.

If one desires to know if a sick person will recover, take nine smooth stones from the running water; fling them over the right shoulder, then lay them in a turf fire to remain untouched for one night. If the disease is to end fatally the stones in the morning will emit a clear sound like a bell when struck together.

Fortune-Telling

Many weird and fearful rites were also practised on Hallow Eve to obtain a knowledge of the future. The hemp seed was sown in the name of the Evil One, and the girls would hang a garment before the fire, and watch from a corner to see the shadowy apparition of the destined husband come down the chimney to turn it; and a ball of yarn was flung from the window, when the apparition would appear below and wind the yarn, while the Paternoster was recited backwards.

In whatever quarter you are looking when you first hear the cuckoo in the season, you will be travelling in that direction before the year is over.

If a cock comes on the threshold and crows, you may expect visitors.

The incantation before the looking-glass was the most fearful of all, for the face of the future husband would appear in the glass, though sometimes a form filled up the surface of the mirror too terrible to describe.

Another practice is to carry the looking-glass outside, and let the rays of the moon fall on the surface, when a face will be revealed, connected for good or evil with the future fate of the holder of the mirror.

The young girls also visit the neighbouring gardens at night, blindfold, to tear up cabbages by the root. If the one first seized is a closed, white cabbage, an old man is the destined husband; but if an open, green head, then a young lover may be hoped for.

Another custom is to make a cake of yellow clay taken from a churchyard, then stick twelve pieces of candle in it, and, kneeling down, recite a form of witch-prayer while all the candles are lighted, and a name is given to each one of them. According as the lights burn out, so will the fate be of the person whose name it bears, and the first that is extinguished betokens death.

They also make a cake of flour, mixed with soot and a spoonful of salt, bake it, and eat it. It will cause thirst, and if a man offers a drink at the time, the girl will assuredly be married before the year is out.

The young girls sometimes rake out the ashes of the fire overnight, making a perfectly flat surface on the hearth. In the morning the print of a foot will be found distinctly marked in the ashes.

If the impress is perfectly flat, it indicates marriage and a long life; but if the toes are bent down into the ashes, death will inevitably follow.

To know the name of the person you are destined to marry, put a snail on a plate of flour—cover it over and leave it all night; in the morning the initial letter of the name will be found traced on the flour by the snail.

Should the snail be quite within his house when you take him up, your lover will be rich; but should the snail almost be out of his shell, then your future husband will be poor, and probably will have no house or home to take you to when you wed him.

If a ball of worsted is thrown into a lime-kiln and wound up till the end is caught by invisible hands, the person who winds it calls out, "Who holds the ball?" The answer will be the name of the future husband or wife. But the experiment must be made only at midnight, and in silence and alone.

Dreams

To dream of a hearse with white plumes is a wedding; but to dream of a wedding is grief, and death will follow.

To dream of a woman kissing you is deceit; but of a man, friendship; and to dream of a horse is exceedingly lucky.

To dream of a priest is bad; even to dream of the devil is better. Remember, also, either a present or a purchase from a priest is unlucky.

Never tell your dreams fasting, and always tell them first to a woman called Mary.

SUPERSTITIONS,
SECRETS,
MAGICAL
PLACES

here is a book, a little book, and the house which has it will never be burned; the ship that holds it will never founder; the woman who keeps it in her hand will be safe in childbirth. But none except a fairy man knows the name of the book, and he will not reveal it for love or money; only on his death-bed will he tell the secret of the name to the one person he selects.

The adepts and fairy doctors keep their mysteries very secret, and it is not easy to discover the word of a charm, for the operator loses his power if the words are said without the proper preliminaries, or if said by a profane person without faith, for the operator should not have uttered the mystery in the hearing of one who would mock, or treat the matter lightly; therefore he is punished.

Some years ago an old man lived in Mayo who had great knowledge of charms, and of certain love philtres that no woman could resist. But before his death he enclosed the written charms in a strong iron box, with directions that no one was to dare to open it except the eldest son of an eldest son in a direct line from himself.

Some people pretend that they have read the charms; and one of them has the strange power to make every one in the house begin to dance, and they can never cease dancing till another spell has been said over them.

But the guardian of the iron box is the only one who knows the magic secret of the spell, and he exacts a good price before he utters it, and so reveals or destroys the witchcraft of the dance.

A sick person's bed must be placed north and south, not crossways.

When a family has been carried off by fever, the house where they died may be again inhabited with safety if a certain number of sheep are driven in to sleep there for three nights.

An iron ring worn on the fourth finger was considered effective against rheumatism by the Irish peasantry from ancient times.

A piece of linen wrap taken from a corpse will cure the swelling of a limb if tied round the part affected.

The ancient arrowheads, called elf-stones by the people, are used as charms to guard the cattle.

People ought to remember that egg-shells are favourite retreats of the fairies, therefore the judicious eater should always break the shell after use, to prevent the fairy sprite from taking up his lodgment therein.

After being cured from a sickness, take an oath never to comb the hair on a Friday, so that the memory of the grace received may remain by this sign till your death. Or whenever you first see the new moon, kneel down and say an ave and a pater; this also is for memory of grace done.

In some parts of Ireland the people, it is said, on first seeing the new moon, fall on their knees and address her in a loud voice with the prayer: "O moon; leave us well as thou hast found us!"

If pursued at night by an evil spirit, or the ghost of one dead, and you hear footsteps behind you, try and reach a stream of running water, for if you can cross it, no devil or ghost will be able to follow you.

If you want a person to win at cards, stick a crooked pin in his coat.

There is one hour in every day when whatever you wish will be granted, but no one knows what that hour is. It is all a chance if we come on it. There is also one hour in the day when ghost-seers can see spirits—but only one—at no other time have they the power, yet they never know the hour, the coming of it is a mystery.

A married woman should not walk upon graves, or her child will have a club-foot. If by accident she treads on a grave she must instantly kneel down, say a prayer, and make a sign of the cross on the sole of her shoe three times over.

The cause of a club-foot is this—The mother stood on a cross in a churchyard before her child was born—so evil came.

Never taken an infant in your arms, nor turn your head to look at it without saying, "God bless it." This keeps away the fatal influence of the Evil Eye.

If a bride steers a boat on the day of her marriage, the winds and the waves have no power over it, be the tempest ever so fierce or the stream ever so rapid.

Fire is the holiest of all things. Walk three times round a fire on St. John's Eve, and you will be safe from disease for all that year.

The cuttings of your hair should not be thrown where birds can find them; for they will take them to build their nests, and then you will have headaches all the year after.

When taking possession of a new house, every one should bring in some present, however trifling, but nothing should be taken away, and a prayer should be said in each corner of your bedroom, and some article of your clothing be deposited there at the same time.

A whitethorn stick is a very unlucky companion on a journey; but a hazel switch brings good luck and has power over the devil.

When taking possession of a new house, every one should bring in some present, however trifling, but nothing should be taken away, and a prayer should be said in each corner of your bedroom, and some article of your clothing be deposited there at the same time.

Never cut an infant's nails till it is a twelve-month old, or it will be light-fingered, and addicted to stealing.

Never get married in harvest, or you will have no rest from worries and troubles, and will always be overworked, and laden with cares and anxieties all your life long.

A new-married couple should retire to rest at the same time, for if the bride were left alone, the fairies would come and steal her away for the sake of her fine clothes.

There are so many superstitions prevalent in the Western Islands which are implicitly believed and acted on. Fishermen when going to sea must always enter the boat by the right side, no matter how inconvenient.

People born in the morning cannot see spirits or the fairy world; but those born at night have power over ghosts, and can see the spirits of the dead.

The seventh son of a seventh son has power over all diseases, and can cure them by laying on of hands; and a son born after his father's death has power over fevers.

The shoe of a horse or of an ass nailed to the door-post will bring good luck; because these animals were in the stall when Christ was born, and are blessed for evermore. But the shoe must be found, not given, in order to bring luck.

A sick person must not be visited on a Friday, nor by any person who has just quitted a wake and looked upon the dead. The hair and nails of a sick person must not be cut till after recovery.

The first days of the year and of the week are the luckiest.

Some days are unlucky to certain families—as Tuesday to the Tudors. Henry VIII, Edward, Mary, and Elizabeth all died upon a Tuesday.

Fridays

It is good to cut the hair at the new moon, and by the light of the moon itself; but never should the hair be cut on a Friday, for it is the most unlucky day of all the year, and no one should begin a journey, or move into a new house, or commence business, or cut out a new dress on a Friday; and, above all, never bring a cat from one house to another on a Friday.

The creation of Adam, the Fall, the expulsion from Eden, and the death of Christ, all took place on a Friday; hence its evil repute and fatal influence, above all other days of the week, upon human actions. But the fairies have great power on that day, and mortals should stay at home after sunset, for the fairies always hold their revels upon Fridays, and resent being interfered with or troubled by the human presence.

Beware of speaking ill of fairies on Friday, because they are present and will work some evil if offended.

Saturdays

Never remove from a house or leave a situation on Saturday.

Never begin to make a dress on Saturday, or the wearer will die within the year.

Never begin a journey on a Friday or Saturday, nor move from your residence, nor change a situation.

Changelings

When a woman first takes ill in her confinement, unlock instantly every press and drawer in the house, but when the child is born, lock them all up again at once, for if care is not taken the fairies will get in and hide in the drawers and presses, to be ready to steal away the little mortal baby when they get the opportunity, and place some ugly, wizened changeling in the cradle beside the poor mother. Therefore every key should be turned, every lock made fast; and if the fairies are hidden inside, let them stay there until all danger is over for the baby by the proper precautions being taken, such as a red coal set under the cradle, and a branch of mountain ash tied over it, or of the alder-tree, according to the sex of the child, for both trees have mystic virtues, probably because of the ancient superstition that the first man was created from an alder-tree, and the first woman from the mountain ash.

The fairies, however, are sometimes successful in carrying off a baby, and the mother finds in the morning a poor weakly little sprite in the cradle in place of her own splendid child. But should the mortal infant happen to grow up ugly, the fairies send it back, for they love beauty above all things; and the fairy chiefs greatly desire a handsome mortal wife, so that a handsome girl must be well guarded, or they will carry her off. The children of such unions grow up beautiful and clever, but are also wild, reckless and extravagant. They are known at once by the beauty of their eyes and hair, and they have a magic fascination that no one can resist, and also a fairy gift of music and song.

Unbaptized Children

Unbaptized children are readily seized by the fairies. The best preventive is a little salt tied up in the child's dress when it is laid to sleep in the cradle.

It is not safe to take an unbaptized child in your arms without making the sign of the cross over it.

It is unlucky to give a coal of fire out of the house before the child is baptized. And a piece of iron should be sewn in the infant's clothes, and kept there till after the baptism.

If three drops of water are given to an infant before it is baptized, it will answer the first three questions put to it.

If a living worm is put into the hand of a child before he is baptized, and kept there till the worm is dead, that child will have power in after life to cure all diseases to which children are subject.

Relics

If a false oath is taken upon a relic the vengeance of God falls upon the swearer, and the doom that few can bear and live rests upon him and upon all his descendants even to the seventh generation. They are shunned by the people, and looked upon as unlucky and accursed. There are some living even now from whom the curse of the past is not lifted, because the seventh generation has not yet passed by.

The Holy Wells

There is no superstition stronger in Ireland than a belief in the curative power of the sacred wells that are scattered over the country; fountains of health and healing some saint had blessed, or by which some saint had dwelt in the far-off ancient times. But well-worship is even older than Christianity. It is part of the early ritual of humanity, brought from the Eastern lands by the first Aryan tribes who migrated westward, passing along from the Mediterranean to the Atlantic shores.

The Delphic oracle in its origin was nothing more than a holy well, shadowed by trees, on which were hung the votive offerings of the praying peasants, long before the rival Kings brought to the sacred spot their votive tributes of silver and gold, and crowns of precious stones.

In Ireland the beautiful, picturesque, and tree-shadowed wells of the country were held sacred by the Druid priests, as is evident from the many remarkable Druidical remains that have been found in their vicinity—ruins of temples and pillar-stones, and stones with strange carvings. Much also of the ancient Druidic ceremonial has been preserved by the people, such as the symbolic dances, the traditions of sun-worship, and other pagan rites, which were incorporated into the Christian ritual of well-worship by the early converts, and are still retained, though, through the lapse of ages, they have entirely lost their original significance, and are now only practised as ancient customs, for which the Irish have great reverence, as having come down to them from their forefathers. The ceremonial is the same at all these places of devout pilgrimage. The pilgrims go round the well a certain number of times, either three or nine, creeping on their hands and knees, but always from east to west, following the apparent motion of the sun, and reciting paters and aves all the time. At the close of each round they built up a small pile of stones; for at the last day the angels will reckon these stones, and he who has said the most prayers will have the highest place in heaven, each saint keeping count for his own votaries. The patient then descends the broken steps to the well and, kneeling down, bathes his forehead and hands in the water, after which oblation the pain or disease he suffered from will be gradually removed, and depart from him for evermore.

At some wells there is often a rude stone monument of the ancient times, and the eyes of the pilgrim must be kept steadily fixed on it while reciting the prayers.

Whenever a white-thorn or an ash-tree shadows the place, the well is held to be peculiarly sacred; and on leaving, having first drunk of the water, the patient ties a votive offering to the branches—generally a coloured handkerchief or a bright red strip cut from a garment; and these offerings are never removed. They remain for years fluttering in the wind and the rain, just as travellers have described the votive offerings on the sacred trees that shadow the holy wells of Persia. They are signs and tokens of gratitude to the patron saint, and are meant to show the devil that he has no longer power to harm the praying pilgrim, or torment him with pains and aches as heretofore. It is not supposed that the water of the well has any natural medicinal properties. The curative efficacy is wholly due to the observance of the ritual in honour of the saint, whose spirit and influence is still over the well, by which he lived, and of which he drank while living on the earth.

The White Stones

At many of the wells quantities of beautiful white stones are found that glitter in the sun, and these are highly esteemed by the pilgrims to build up their prayer monuments.

One day some women were eagerly collecting these stones, after each round of praying, in order to build up a monument; when suddenly a strain of soft, exquisite music seemed to rise up from the water and float by them. In their joy and wonder the women clapped their hands and laughed aloud, when instantly the music ceased and the pile of stones fell down. By which sign they knew that they should not have laughed while the angels were singing; and they fell on their knees and prayed.

A holy well once lost all its power because a murder had been committed near it; and another because it was cursed by a priest in consequence of the immorality that prevailed at the patterns.

The Sacred Trout

The water of the sacred well must never be used for household purposes—cooking, washing, or the like. But after the well was cursed by the priest, and the tents were struck, and no pattern was held there any longer, it lost all its sanctity, and was no longer held sacred by the people, who began to fill their pails, and carry the water away from home for cooking and household use; while also they all washed their clothes down at the well, just as if no sanctity had ever been in the water.

However, one day a woman having put down a pot of water to boil, found that no amount of fire would heat it. Still it remained ice-cold, as if just drawn from the well. So she looked carefully into the pot, and there beheld the Sacred Speckled Trout sailing round and round quite contented and happy. On seeing this, she knew that the curse was lifted from the well, and she ran and told the priest. His reverence having seen the Sacred Trout with his own eyes, ordered it to be carried back to the well, the water of which at once regained all its sacred powers by the blessing of the priest; and he gave the people leave thenceforth to hold their pattern there, so as they have behaved themselves like decent, God-fearing Christians for the future. But the water was not allowed to be carried away any more to their houses for household purposes; the desecration of the holy water of a sacred well being strictly forbidden as dangerous and unlucky.

Ancient Mysteries

The ancient Druids, priests, and magi possessed many wonderful secrets. The priest, by waving of his wand, could throw a person into a deep sleep, and while under the influence of this Druidical operation, the patient could describe what was passing at a distance, and exhibit all the phenomena of clairvoyance as known to the moderns. The magi had also the power of prolonging life, and for this purpose an Irish pearl was swallowed, which rendered the swallower as youthful as when in his prime.

The Druids believed that the moon exercised a powerful influence over the human frame, and produced a violent pulsation in the blood-vessels during the space of twenty-four hours.

It is reported that the ancient Irish used poisoned weapons, and the poison was extracted from hellebore and the berries of the yew tree.

It is believed that if any of the Irish of noble race should die abroad, the dead are so anxious to rest in the ancestral home, that their dust flies on the winds of heaven over land and sea, blasting every green and living thing in its passage as it goes by, until it reaches the hereditary burial ground, and there rests in peace. And this fatal and baneful rush of the dust of the dead, which blights the crops and the fruit, is called by the people, "The red wind of the hills," and is held by them in the utmost dread.

PROVERBS—
POPULAR
WISDOM

vast amount of characteristic popular wisdom has existed for ages amongst the Irish peasantry, condensed in proverbial sayings that show a subtle insight into motives and conduct, with a deep knowledge of all the varied influences that stir the human heart; but though well worthy of a place in our national literature, these proverbs of the people have remained unknown to the general reader, from the fact of their being hidden away in the obscurity of the original vernacular. This hindrance, however, has now, to a great extent, been removed; for, within the last few decades, several eminent Celtic scholars have taken up the subject, and devoted both time and learning, with patient, loving zeal, to the collection and translation into English of many of those interesting examples of ancient thought—the result being that many hundred Irish proverbs have now been rescued from obscurity and made known to English literature.

National proverbs form a kind of synthesis of national character and of the moral tendencies of a race. There may be no written code amongst the peasantry of morals or manners, yet deeper truths concerning human actions, motives, and tendencies often lie at the base of the popular proverbs, than could be gathered from even the most learned and diffuse essays of the philosopher.

Irish proverbs are especially remarkable for their concise and forcible expression of truths concerning life, conduct, and action. The matured wisdom of the centuries is in them, and they bear witness to the acute vision of the ancient seers and Fileas, who could fathom the very depths of the human soul, and reveal the mysteries of life in these strong, enduring maxims of steadfast truth. A keen sense, also, of the sad and bitter realities of human destiny is observable in them—the result of shrewd observation, shadowed by the melancholy of age and experience.

The peasants rarely speak on any subject that touches them deeply without illustrating their opinions by a proverb, uttered with the firm decision of assured conviction. Indeed, the peculiar veneration in which the Irish hold the sacred wisdom of their ancestors has given rise to the saying, "It is impossible to contradict the old word" (the proverb).

The Irish people have always believed that their Kings,

Brehons, Ollamhs, and Bards were gifted with singular and peculiar intelligence, and a mystic power of reading the secrets of the heart. Hence the sayings of these great wise men of ancient renown have passed through the mind of the people in each successive generation, and are still for ever on their lips as so many sacred maxims, to be accepted, without questioning, as undeniable truths respecting their life, words, and works; for many of these proverbs show, in a marked manner, the still ineffaceable peculiarities of Irish nature—the kindness and sensitiveness of the people, their instinctive sense of the grace of courtesy of manner, their love of distinction, their trust in good luck rather than in work, their eminently social qualities, especially the love of conversation, and the pathetic acceptance of the doom that want and poverty bring on life, "because it is the will of God."

These qualities have been connected with the Irish race throughout all history, and are as true now, in the present time, as they have been in the past. Above a hundred years ago, Lord Macartney, the great Ambassador of England to the East, thus described the native Irish: "They are active in body; bold and daring; patient of cold, hunger, and fatigue; dauntless in danger, and regardless of life when glory is in view; warm in love and friendship, quick in resentment, and implacable in hatred; generous and hospitable beyond all bounds of prudence; credulous, superstitious, and vain; talkative, disputatious, and strongly disposed to turbulence and contest. They are all fond of learning, and are endowed with excellent parts, but are usually more remarkable for liveliness of thought than accuracy of expression."

Many of these national and enduring race characteristics will be found expressed with much force and freedom in the following selections from the terse and acute sayings of ancient Irish wisdom.

True greatness knows gentleness.

When wrathful words arise a closed mouth is soothing.

Have a mouth of ivy and a heart of holly.

A silent mouth is musical.

Associate with the nobles, but be not cold to the poor and lowly.

A constant guest is never welcome.

A short visit is best, and that not too often, even to the house of a friend.

Blind should be the eyes in the abode of another.

Great minds live apart; people may meet, but the mountains and the rocks never.

A man with loud talk makes truth itself seem folly.

Much loquacity brings a man's good sense into disrepute, and by a superfluity of words, truth is obscured.

Neither praise nor dispraise thyself; the well bred are always modest.

It is difficult to soothe the proud.

Every nursling as it is nursed; every web as it is woven.

Without store no friends; without rearing no manners.

A little friendship is better than much friendship.

Gentleness is better than haughtiness.

Tell not your complaints to him who has no pity.

The peacemaker is never in the way.

Forsake not a friend of many years for the acquaintance of a day.

No heat like that of shame.

No pain like that of refusal.

No sorrow like the loss of friends.

No feast till there is the roast.

No galling trial till one gets married.

Praise youth, and it will advance to success.

Reputation is more enduring than life.

Wine is pleasant, unpleasant the price.

Drinking is the brother of robbery.

Character is better than wealth.

If the head cannot bear the glory of the crown, better be without it.

Face the sun, but turn your back to the storm.

Without money fame is dead.

He who is up is extolled; he who is down is trampled on.

Sweet is the voice of the man who has wealth, but the voice of the indigent man is harsh—no one heeds him.

How many mourn the want of possessions; yet the strong, the brave, and the rich, all go to the grave at last; like the poor, and the emaciated, and the infant.

Death is the poor man's best physician.

Many a day we shall rest in the clay.

A hound's tooth, a thorn in the hand, and a fool's retort are the three sharpest things of all.

The lake is not encumbered by the swan; nor the steed by the bridle; nor the sheep by the wool; nor the man by the soul that is in him.

Conversation is the cure for every sorrow. Even contention is better than loneliness.

Bad is a bad servant, but he is better than none.

It is sad to have no friend; sad to have unfortunate children; sad to have only a poor hut; but sadder to have nothing good or bad.

Idleness is a fool's desire.

Do not take the thatch from your own roof to buy slates for another man's house.

The tree remains, but not the hand that planted it.

A heavy purse makes a light heart.

Better April showers than the breadth of the ocean in gold.

Never count your crops till June is over.

Autumn days come quickly, like the running of a hound upon the moor.

Send round the glass to the south, from the left to the right hand; all things should front the south.

A meeting in the sunlight is lucky, and a burying in the rain.

Winter comes fast on the lazy.

The beginning of a ship is a board; of a kiln, a stone; of a king's reign, salutation; and the beginning of health is sleep.

Have sense, patience, and self-restraint, and no mischief will come.

Better a good run than a long standing.

Falling is easier than rising.

One morsel of a rabbit is worth two of a cat.

Cleverness is better than strength.

Good fortune often abides with a fool.

If the day is long, night comes at last.

There is no joy without affliction.

No one seeks relationship to the unfortunate.

A foot at rest meets nothing.

The day of storm is not the day for thatching.

Virtue is everlasting wealth.

Avarice is the foundation of every evil.

Wisdom excels all riches.

An empty vessel has the greatest sound.

Three good things are often thrown away: A good thing done for an old man, for an ill-natured man, or for a child; for the old man dies, the other is false, and the child forgets.

God never closed one gap but He opened another.

Good begets goodness, and bad badness. Money begets money, and wealth friendship.

Gentleness is better than haughtiness; adjustment than going to law. A small house and full store, then a large house and little food.

The son of a widow who has plenty of cattle, the foal of an old mare at grass, and the miller's dog who has always plenty of meal, are the three happiest creatures living.

Better to spare in time than out of time.

In slender currents comes good luck; in rolling torrents comes misfortune.

Misfortune follows fortune inch by inch.

Good luck is better than early rising.

It is better to be lucky than wise.

Every man has bad luck awaiting him some time or other. But leave the bad luck to the last; perchance it may never come.

Have a kind look for misery, but a frown for an enemy.

A misty winter brings a pleasant spring. A pleasant winter a misty spring.

A poem ought to be well made at first, for there is many a one to spoil it afterwards.

Red in the South means rain and cold.

Red in the East is a sign of frost.

Red in the North rain and wind.

Red in the West sunshine and thaw.

You will live during the year, for we were just speaking of you.

There is wisdom in the raven's head.

A man may be his own ruin. It is a wedge from itself that splits the oak-tree.

Want, slavery, scarcity of provisions, plagues, battles, conflicts, defeat in battle, inclement weather, rapine, from the unworthiness of a prince do spring.

In contradistinction to this statement, the reign of a good prince, it is asserted, brings a blessing on the land. In the time of Cormac-Mac-Art, "The world was delightful and happy, nine nuts grew on each twig, and nine sure twigs on each rod." And in the reign of Cathal-Crovh-dhearg, "The grass was so abundant that it reached above the horns of the cattle, when they lay down to rest in the field."

BELIEFS ABOUT ANIMALS

here are no traces in Irish legend of animal worship, but many concerning the influence of animals upon human life, and of their interference with human affairs.

The peasants believe that the domestic animals know all about us, especially the dog and the cat. They listen to everything that is said; they watch the expression of the face, and can even read the thoughts. The Irish say it is not safe to ask a question of a dog, for he may answer, and should he do so the questioner will surely die.

The position of the animal race in the life scheme is certainly full of mystery. Gifted with extraordinary intelligence, yet with dumb souls vainly struggling for utterance, they seem like prisoned spirits in bondage, suffering the punishment, perhaps, for sin in some former human life, and now waiting the completion of the cycle of expiation that will advance them again to the human state.

Concerning Dogs

Some very weird superstitions exist in Ireland concerning the howlings of dogs. If a dog is heard to howl near the house of a sick person, all hope of his recovery is given up, and the patient himself sinks into despair, knowing that his doom is sealed. But the Irish are not alone in holding this superstition. The Egyptians, Hebrews, Greeks, and Romans all looked on the howling of the dog as ominous.

The howling of the dog was considered by these nations as the first note of the funeral dirge and the signal that the coming of death was near.

But the origin of the superstition may be traced back to Egypt, where dogs and dog-faced gods were objects of worship; probably because Sirius, the Dog-star, appeared precisely before the rising of the Nile, and thereby gave the people a mystic and supernatural warning to prepare for the overflow.

This strange superstition concerning the howling of dogs, when, as is supposed, they are conscious of the approach of the Spirit of Death, and see him though he is shrouded and invisible to human eyes, may be found pervading the legends of all nations

from the earliest period down to the present time; for it still exists in full force amongst all classes, the educated, as well as the unlettered peasantry; and to this day the howling of a dog where a sick person is lying is regarded in Ireland in all grades of society with pale dismay as a certain sign of approaching death.

It is strange and noteworthy that although the dog is so faithful to man, yet it is never mentioned in the Bible without an expression of contempt; and Moses in his code of laws makes the dog an unclean animal, probably to deter the Israelites from the Egyptian worship of this animal. It was the lowest term of offence—"Is thy servant a dog?" False teachers, persecutors, Gentiles, unholy men, and others sunk in sin and vileness were called dogs; while at the same time the strange prophetic power of these animals was universally acknowledged and recognized.

The Romans sacrificed a dog at the Lupercalia in February. And to meet a dog with her whelps was considered in the highest degree unlucky. Of all living creatures the name of "dog" applied to any one expressed the lowest form of insult, contempt, and reproach. Yet, of all animals, the dog has the noblest qualities, the highest intelligence, and the most enduring affection for man.

The word hound entered into many combinations as a name for various animals. Thus the rabbit was called, "the hound of the brake"; the hare was the "brown hound"; the moth was called "the hound of fur," owing to the voracity with which it devoured raiment. And the otter is still called by the Irish *Madradh-Uisgue* (the dog of the water).

The names of most creatures of the animal kingdom were primitive, the result evidently of observation. Thus the hedgehog was named "the ugly little fellow." The ant was the "slender one." The trout, *Breac*, or "the spotted," from the skin. And the wren was called "the Druid bird," because if anyone understood the chirrup, they would have a knowledge of coming events as foretold by the bird.

Concerning Cats

The Irish have always looked on cats as evil and mysteriously connected with some demoniacal influence. On entering a house the usual salutation is, "God save all here, except the cat." Even the cake on the griddle may be blessed, but no one says, "God bless the cat."

It is believed that the devil often assumes the form of these animals. The familiar of a witch is always a black cat; and it is supposed that black cats have powers and faculties quite different from all other of the feline tribe. They are endowed with reason, can understand conversations, and are quite able to talk if they considered it advisable and judicious to join in the conversation. Their temperament is exceedingly unamiable, they are artful, malignant, and skilled in deception, and people should be very cautious in caressing them, for they have the venomous heart and the evil eye, and are ever ready to do an injury. Yet the liver of a black cat has the singular power to excite love when properly administered. If ground to powder and infused into potion, the recipient is fated to love passionately the person who offers it and has worked the charm.

Yet it is singular that the blood of the black cat is esteemed of wonderful power when mixed with herbs, for charms; and also of great efficacy in potions for the cure of disease; but three drops of the blood are sufficient, and it is generally obtained by nipping off a small piece of the tail.

Cat Nature

The observation of cats is very remarkable, and also their intense curiosity. They examine everything in a house, and in a short time know all about it as well as the owner. They are never deceived by stuffed birds, or any such weak human delusions. They fathom it all at one glance, and then turn away with apathetic indifference, as if saying, in cat language—"We know all about it."

But cats are decidedly malefic; they are selfish, revengeful, treacherous, cunning, and generally dangerous. The evil spirit in them is easily aroused. It is an Irish superstition that if you are going a journey, and meet a cat, you should turn back. But the cat must meet you on the road, not simply be in the house; and it must look you full in the face. Then cross yourself and turn back; for a witch or a devil is in your path.

Cats were special objects of mysterious dread to the ancient Irish. They believed that many of them were men and women metamorphosed into cats by demoniacal power. Cats also were the guardians of hidden treasure, and had often great battles among themselves on account of the hidden gold; when a demon, in the shape of the chief cat, led on the opposing forces on each side, and compelled all the cats in the district to take part in the conflict.

The Druidical or royal cat, the chief monarch of all the cats in Ireland, was endowed with human speech and faculties, and possessed great and singular privileges. "A slender black cat, wearing a chain of silver," so it is described.

Concerning Birds

In all countries superstitions of good or evil are attached to certain birds. The raven, for instance, has a wide-world reputation as the harbinger of evil and ill-luck. The wild geese portend a severe winter; the robin is held sacred, for no one would think of harming a bird who bears on his breast the blessed mark of the blood of Christ; while the wren is hunted to death with intense and cruel hate on St. Stephen's Day.

The Magpie

There is no Irish name for the Magpie. It is generally called *Francagh*, a Frenchman, though no one knows why. Many queer tales are narrated of this bird, rising from its quaint ways, its adroit cunning and habits of petty larceny. Its influence is not considered evil, though to meet one alone in the morning when going a journey is an ill omen, but to meet more than one magpie betokens good fortune, according to the old rhyme which runs thus—

> "One for Sorrow,
> Two for Mirth,
> Three for Marriage,
> Four for a Birth."

The Wren

The wren is mortally hated by the Irish; for on one occasion, when the Irish troops were approaching to attack a portion of Cromwell's army, the wrens came and perched on the Irish drums, and by their tapping and noise aroused the English soldiers, who fell on the Irish troops and killed them all. So ever since the Irish hunt the wren on St. Stephen's Day, and teach their children to run it through with thorns and kill it whenever it can be caught. A dead wren was also tied to a pole and carried from house to house by boys, who demanded money; if nothing was given the wren was buried on the door-step, which was considered a great insult to the family and a degradation.

The Raven and Water Wagtail

If ravens come cawing about a house it is a sure sign of death, for the raven is Satan's own bird.

The water-wagtail is particularly disliked, for it has strange mystical powers, and its presence always forebodes something fatal. Yet beware of killing it, for it has three drops of the devil's blood in its little body, and ill-luck ever goes with it, and follows it.

The Cuckoo and Robin Redbreast

It is very unlucky to kill the cuckoo or break its eggs, for it brings fine weather; but most unlucky of all things is to kill the robin redbreast. The robin is God's own bird, sacred and holy, and held in the greatest veneration because of the beautiful tradition current amongst the people, that it was the robin plucked out the sharpest thorn that was piercing Christ's brow on the cross; and in so doing the breast of the bird was dyed red with the Saviour's blood, and so has remained ever since a sacred and blessed sign to preserve the robin from harm and make it beloved of all men.

The first time you hear the cuckoo, look down at your feet; if a hair is lying there you will live to comb your own gray locks at a good old age. There is an old rhyme respecting this bird:

> If a cuckoo sits on a bare thorn,
> You may sell your cow and buy corn;
> But if she sits on a green bough,
> You may sell your corn and buy a cow.

Concerning Living Creatures

The Cricket

The crickets are believed to be enchanted. People do not like to express an exact opinion about them, so they are spoken of with great mystery and awe, and no one would venture to kill them for the whole world. But they are by no means evil; on the contrary, the presence of the cricket is considered lucky, and their singing keeps away the fairies at night, who are always anxious, in their selfish way, to have the whole hearth left clear for themselves, that they may sit round the last embers of the fire, and drink the cup of milk left for them by the farmer's wife, in peace and quietness. The crickets are supposed to be hundreds of years old, and their talk, could we understand it, would no doubt be most interesting and instructive.

The Beetle

The beetle is not killed by the people for the following reason: they have a tradition that one day the chief priests sent messengers in every direction to look for the Lord Jesus, and they came to a field where a man was reaping, and asked him—

"Did Jesus of Nazareth pass this way?"

"No," said the man, "I have not seen him."

"But I know better," said a little cock running up, "for He was here to-day and rested, and has not long gone away."

"That is false," said a great big black beetle, coming forward; "He has not passed since yesterday, and you will never find Him on this road; try another."

So the people kill the cock because he tried to betray Christ; but they spare the beetle and will not touch him, because he saved the Lord on that day.

The Hare

Hares are considered unlucky, as the witches constantly assume their form in order to gain entrance to a field where they can bewitch the cattle. A man once fired at a hare he met in the early morning, and having wounded it, followed the track of the blood till it disappeared within a cabin. On entering he found Nancy Molony, the greatest witch in all the county, sitting by the fire, groaning and holding her side. And then the man knew that she had been out in the form of a hare, and he rejoiced over her discomfiture.

Still it is not lucky to kill a hare before sunrise, even when it crosses your path; but should it cross *three* times, then turn back, for danger is on the road before you.

The Weasel

Weasels are spiteful and malignant, and old withered witches sometimes take this form. It is extremely unlucky to meet a weasel the first thing in the morning; still it would be hazardous to kill it, for it might be a witch and take revenge. Indeed one should be very cautious about killing a weasel at any time, for all the other weasels will resent your audacity, and kill your chickens when an opportunity offers. The only remedy is to kill one chicken yourself, make the sign of the cross solemnly three times over it, then tie it to a stick hung up in the yard, and the weasels will have no more power for evil, nor the witches who take their form, at least during the year, if the stick is left standing; but the chicken may be eaten when the sun goes down.

THE USES OF HERBS

There are seven herbs of great value and power; they are ground ivy, vervain, eyebright, groundsel, foxglove, the bark of the elder-tree, and the young shoots of the hawthorn.

Nine balls of these mixed together may be taken, and afterwards a potion made of bog-water and salt, boiled in a vessel, with a piece of money and an elf-stone. The elf-stone is generally found near a rath; it has great virtues, but being once lifted up by the spade it must never touch the earth, or all its virtue is gone. (This elf-stone is in reality only an ancient stone arrowhead.)

The *Mead Cailleath*, or wood anemone, is used as a plaister for wounds.

The hazel-tree has many virtues. It is sacred and powerful against devils' wiles, and has mysteries and secret properties known to the wise and the adepts.

It was by the use of a hazel wand that St. Patrick drove out the serpents from Ireland, one only escaping, who plunged into the Great Lake at Killarney, and remains there to this day crying to be released. And with a hazel stick a person can draw a circle around himself, within which no evil thing can enter—fairy, or demon, or serpent, or evil spirit. But the stick must be cut on May morning, and before sunrise, to make it powerful.

The ancient Irish believed that there were fountains at the head of the chief rivers of Ireland, over each of which grew nine hazel-trees that at certain times produced beautiful red nuts. These nuts fell on the surface of the water, and the salmon in the river came up and ate of them, which caused the red spots on the salmon. And whoever could catch and eat one of these salmon would be indued with the sublimest poetic intellect. Hence the phrase current amongst the people: "Had I the net of science"; "Had I eaten of the salmon of knowledge." And this supernatural knowledge came to the great Fionn through the touch of a salmon, and made him foreknow all events.

Of all herbs the yarrow is the best for cures and potions. It is even sewn up in clothes as a preventive of disease.

There is an herb, also, or fairy grass, called the *Faud Shaughran*, or the "stray sod," and whoever treads the path it grows on is compelled by an irresistible impulse to travel on without stopping, all through the night, delirious and restless, over bog and mountain, through hedges and ditches, till wearied and bruised and cut, his garments torn, his hands bleeding, he finds himself in the morning twenty or thirty miles, perhaps, from his own home. And those who fall under this strange influence have all the time the sensation of flying and are utterly unable to pause or turn back or change their career. There is, however, another herb that can neutralize the effects of the *Faud Shaughran*, but only the initiated can utilize its mystic properties.

Another grass is the *Fair-Gortha*, or the "hunger-stricken sod," and if the hapless traveller accidentally treads on this grass by the road-side, while passing on a journey, either by night or day, he becomes at once seized with the most extraordinary cravings of hunger and weakness, and unless timely relief is afforded he must certainly die.

All herbs pulled on May Day Eve have a sacred healing power, if pulled in the name of the Holy Trinity; but if in the name of Satan, they work evil. Some herbs are malefic if broken by the hand. So the plant is tied to a dog's foot, and when he runs it breaks, without a hand touching it, and may be used with safety.

A man pulled a certain herb on May Eve to cure his son who was sick to death. The boy recovered, but disappeared and was never heard of after, and the father died that day year. He had broken the fatal herb with the hand and so the doom fell on him.

Another man did the like, and gave the herb to his son to eat, who immediately began to bark like a dog, and so continued till he died.

Pettigrew, in his interesting book on medical superstitions, mentions the ancient idea that black hellebore was to be plucked, not cut, and this with the right hand, which was then covered with the robe, while the herb was secretly conveyed to the left hand. The person gathering it, also, was to be clad in white, and to offer a sacrifice of bread and wine.

Pettigrew also mentions that vervain, one of the sacred herbs of the Irish, was to be gathered on the rising of the Dog-star, when neither sun nor moon was shining, an expiatory sacrifice of fruit and honey being previously offered to the earth. Hence the power of vervain to cure fevers, eradicate poison, and render the possessor invulnerable.

The fatal herbs have signs known only to the fairy doctors, who should always be consulted before treating the sick in the family.

There are *seven* herbs that nothing natural or supernatural can injure; they are vervain, John's-wort, speedwell, eyebright, mallow, yallow, and self-help. But they must be pulled at noon on a bright day, near the full moon, to have full power.

It is firmly believed that the herb-women who perform curses receive their knowledge from the fairies, who impart to them the mystical secrets of herbs and where to find them; but these secrets must not be revealed except on the death-bed, and then only to the eldest of the family. Many mysterious rites are practised in the making and the giving of potions; and the messenger who carries the draught to the sufferer must never look behind him nor utter a word till he hands the medicine to the patient, who instantly swallows a cup of the mixture before other hands have touched it.

The yew-tree, the ash, and the elder-tree were sacred.

The willow is thought to have a soul in it which speaks in music; for this reason the Irish harps were generally made of the wood. Brian Borohm's ancient harp, still in existence, is made of the willow tree.

The juice of deadly night-shade distilled, and given in a drink, will make the person who drinks believe whatever you will to tell him, and choose him to believe.

When children are pining away, they are supposed to be fairy-struck; and the juice of twelve leaves of foxglove may be given: also in cases of fever the same.

A bunch of mint tied round the wrist keeps off infection and disease.

The rowan tree is very sacred, and branches of it should be hung on May morning over the child's cradle, and over the churn and the door, to keep away evil spirits and evil hands.

Whoever has the four-leaved shamrock has good luck in all things. He cannot be cheated in a bargain, nor deceived, and whatever he undertakes will prosper. It enlightens the brain, and makes one see and know the truth; and by its aid wondrous things can be done. So the people say: "Whoever has the four-leaved shamrock can work miracles." But it must never be shown to man nor mortal, or the power would exist no more.

Great virtue is attributed to the briar, especially in cases of a sprain, or dislocation; the species bearing a reddish flower being the best for use.

The buds of the briar are used in spring to make a refreshing drink for the sick, and the roots in winter. The roots are boiled for twelve hours in an earthen vessel, then a small cupful of the liquid is administered frequently to the patient, who, after some time, falls into a deep sleep from which he will awake perfectly cured.

THE FAIRY
RACE

rom the earliest ages the world has believed in the existence of a race midway between the angel and man, gifted with power to exercise a strange mysterious influence over human destiny. The Persians called this mystic race Peris; the Egyptians and the Greeks named them demons, not as evil, but as mysterious allies of man, invisible though ever present; capable of kind acts but implacable if offended.

The Irish called them the Sidhe, or spirit-race, or the *Feadh-Ree*, a modification of the word Peri. Their country is the *Tirna-oge*, the land of perpetual youth, where they live a life of joy and beauty, never knowing disease or death, which is not to come on them till the judgment day, when they are fated to pass into annihilation, to perish utterly and be seen no more. They can assume any form and they make horses out of bits of straw, on which they ride over the country, and to Scotland and back. They have no religion, but a great dread of the *Scapular* (Latin words from the Gospels written by a priest and hung round the neck). Their power is great over unbaptized children, and such generally grow up evil and have the evil eye, and bring ill luck, unless the name of God is instantly invoked when they look at any one fixedly and in silence.

All over Ireland the fairies have the reputation of being very beautiful, with long yellow hair sweeping the ground, and lithe light forms. They love milk and honey, and sip the nectar from the cups of flowers, which is their fairy wine.

Underneath the lakes, and deep down in the heart of the hills, they have their fairy palaces of pearl and gold, where they live in splendour and luxury, with music and song and dancing and laughter and all joyous things as befits the gods of the earth. If our eyes were touched by a fairy salve we could see them dancing on the hill in the moonlight. They are served on vessels of gold, and each fairy chief, to mark his rank, wears a circlet of gold round his head.

The Sidhe race were once angels in heaven, but were cast out as a punishment for their pride. Some fell to earth, others were cast into the sea, while many were seized by demons and carried down to hell, whence they issue as evil spirits, to tempt men to destruction under various disguises; chiefly, however, as beautiful young maidens, endowed with the power of song and gifted with the most enchanting wiles. Under the influence of these beautiful sirens a man will commit any and every crime. Then when his soul is utterly black they carry him down to hell, where he remains forever tortured by the demons to whom he sold himself.

The fairies are very numerous, more numerous than the human race. In their palaces underneath the hills and in the lakes and the sea they hide away much treasure. All the treasure of wrecked ships is theirs; and all the gold that men have hidden and buried in the earth when danger was on them, and then died and left no sign of the place to their descendants. And all the gold of the mine and the jewels of the rocks belong to them; and in the Sifra, or fairy-house, the walls are silver and the pavement is gold, and the banquet-hall is lit by the glitter of the diamonds that stud the rocks.

If you walk nine times round a fairy rath at the full of the moon, you will find the entrance to the Sifra; but if you enter, beware of eating the fairy food or drinking the fairy wine. The Sidhe will, indeed, wile and draw many a young man into the fairy dance, for the fairy women are beautiful, so beautiful that a man's eyes grow dazzled who looks on them, with their long hair floating like the ripe golden corn and their robes of silver gossamer; they have perfect forms, and their dancing is beyond all expression graceful; but if a man is tempted to kiss a *Sighoge*, or young fairy spirit, in the dance, he is lost forever—the madness of love will fall on him, and he will never again be able to return to earth or to leave the enchanted fairy palace. He is dead to his kindred and race for ever more.

On Fridays the fairies have special power over all things, and chiefly on that day they select and carry off the young mortal girls as brides for the fairy chiefs. But after seven years, when the girls grow old and ugly, they send them back to their kindred, giving them, however, as compensation, a knowledge of herbs and philtres and secret spells, by which they can kill or cure, and have power over men both for good and evil.

The fairies are passionately fond of music; it is therefore dangerous for a young girl to sing when she is all alone by the lake, for the spirits will draw her down to them to sing to them in the fairy palace under the waves, and her people will see her no more.

The Nature of Fairies

In Connaught the people have many strange superstitions of great antiquity. If a child spills its tin of milk on the ground, the mother says: "That to the fairies, leave it to them and welcome," and the child is never scolded, lest that might bring ill luck. For the fairies hate everything that looks mean and niggardly, being themselves of a bright, free, joyous nature; except, indeed the Banshee, who is the spirit of sorrow and doom.

And the fairies like people who are kind and considerate, and who leave food on the dresser and fire in the grate at night for them when they hold their councils; yet not too much fire, for they dislike smoke, and the good woman of the house must never throw out water after dark, without saying: "Take care of the water"; for the fairies are very nice in their ways, and resent any such awkward chance as might spoil their pretty gay caps and feathers. They also greatly desire human aid, and are very clever and acute in obtaining it.

The fairies may be propitiated, but are never worshipped by the people, who look on them as inferior beings to themselves; and they know well that all the fairy spite against them is caused by envy and jealousy because man has been created immortal, while the Sidhe race is doomed to extinction at the last day. But saints and angels receive full homage from the people, and they are invoked against all evil influences with the most earnest faith and trust.

Fairy Doctors

The fairy doctors are generally females. Old women, especially, are considered to have peculiar mystic and supernatural power. They cure chiefly by charms and incantations, transmitted by tradition through many generations; and by herbs, of which they have a surprising knowledge.

The fairies have an aversion to the sight of blood; and the peasants, therefore, have a great objection to being bled, lest "the good people" would be angry. Besides, they have much more faith in charms and incantations than in any dispensary doctor that ever practised amongst them.

Sprites and Spirits

The Banshee

The Ban-Sidhe, the fairy spirit of doom, never appears but to aristocrats. She is an appanage only of the highest families, who are always followed by the shadow of this spirit of death, supposed to be a beautiful young girl of the race, who cannot enter heaven until some other member of the family, who must be likewise young and beautiful, takes her place through death. Ban, or Van, means woman; and *Vanitha*, the lady of the house, in Sanscrit, as in Irish, comes from the root *Van*—to love, to desire. To this day the lady of the house is called *The Vanitha* by the Irish, the word having the same meaning as Venus, "the loved one," in its original signification.

At Lord O'Neil's residence, Shane's Castle, there is a room appropriated to the use of the Banshee, and she often appears there; sometimes shrouded and muffled in a dark, mist-like cloak. At other times, she is seen as a beautiful young girl, with long, red-gold hair, and wearing a green kirtle and scarlet mantle, brooched with gold, after the Irish fashion.

There is no harm or fear of evil in her mere presence, unless she is seen in the act of crying; but this is a fatal sign, and the mournful wail is a sure and certain prophecy that the angel of death is waiting for one of the family.

The Leprehaun

The little gray Leprehaun has the secret of hidden gold, and by the power of a certain herb he can discover it and thus become master of unlimited wealth. But no one has ever yet obtained from the tricksy little sprite the name of the herb or the words of the charm which reveal the hidden treasure, only the Leprehaun has the knowledge.

There are also herbs of grace to be gathered on May morning which give wealth to him who knows the proper form of incantation; but if he reveals the mystery he dies. So the adepts keep the secret, being afraid of the doom. Yet the peasantry still make constant efforts to find the hidden gold, and many curious rites are practised by them to obtain a knowledge of the mystic herbs.

The Demon Bride

The ancient churchyard of Truagh, County Monaghan, is said to be haunted by an evil spirit, whose appearance generally forebodes death.

The legend runs that at funerals the spirit watches for the person who remains last in the graveyard. If it be a young man who is there alone, the spirit takes the form of a beautiful young girl, inspires him with an ardent passion, and exacts a promise that he will meet her that day month in the churchyard. The promise is then sealed by a kiss, which sends a fatal fire through his veins, so that he is unable to resist her caresses, and makes the promise required. Then she disappears, and the young man proceeds homewards; but no sooner has he passed the boundary wall of the churchyard, than the whole story of the evil spirit rushes on his mind, and he knows that he has sold himself, soul and body, for a demon's kiss. The terror and dismay take hold of him, till despair becomes insanity, and on the very day month fixed for the meeting with the demon bride, the victim dies the death of a raving lunatic, and is laid in the fatal graveyard of Truagh.

But the evil spirit does not limit its operations to the graveyard; for sometimes the beautiful demon form appears at weddings or festivities, and never fails to secure its victims, by dancing them into the fever that maddens the brain, and too surely ends in death.

TRADITIONS—
THE FOLK DAYS

ay Day in old time was the period of greatest rejoicing in Ireland, a festival of dances and garlands to celebrate the Resurrection of Nature, as November was a time of solemn gloom and mourning for the dying sun; for the year was divided into these two epochs, symbolising death and resurrection, and the year itself was expressed by a word meaning "the circle of the sun," the symbol of which was a hoop, always carried in the popular processions, wreathed with the rowan and the marsh marigold, and bearing, suspended within it, two balls to represent the sun and moon, sometimes covered with gold and silver paper.

A number of ancient traditions circle especially around May Day, called in Irish *La-Bel-Taine* (the day of the sacred Baal fire). In the old pagan times, on May Eve, the Druids lit the great sacred fire at Tara, and as the signal flames rose up high in the air, a fire was kindled on every hill in Erin, till the whole island was circled by a zone of flame. It is a saying amongst the Irish, "Fire and salt are the two most precious things given to man." Fire, above all, was held sacred by them, as the symbol of Deity and the mystic means of purification, and three things were never given away by them on May Day—fire, milk, or butter—for this would be to give away luck. No one was permitted to carry a lighted sod out of the house, or to borrow fire in any way. And no strange hand was allowed to milk the cow, for if the first can were filled in the name of the devil there would be no more milk that year for the family—it would all be secretly taken away by the fairies.

The First Three Days of May

The first three days of May were very dangerous to cattle, for the fairies had then great power given them of the Evil One; therefore they were well guarded by lighted fires and branches of the rowan, and the milkmaid made the sign of the Cross after milking, with the froth of the milk. Nothing else was so effective against witches and demons.

During the first three days of May, also, it was necessary to take great precautions against the fairies entering the house, for if once they gained admittance they worked mischief. They would come disguised as old women or wayfarers in order to steal a burning coal—a most fatal theft—or to carry off the herbs of power, that were always gathered on May morning with the dew on them. But the best preventive against fairy or demon power was to scatter primroses on the threshold, for no fairy could pass the flower, and the house and household were left in peace, though all strangers were looked upon with great suspicion.

Many of the old customs still remain among the peasants. Among others it is thought right and proper to have the threshold swept clean on May Eve. Ashes are then lightly sprinkled over it, and in the morning the print of a foot is looked for. If it turn inward a marriage is certain, but if outward then a death will happen in the family before the year is out.

The cattle also are still singed along the back with a lighted wisp of straw, and a bunch of primroses is tied to the cow's tail, for the evil spirits cannot touch anything guarded by these flowers, if they are plucked before sunrise, not else.

But the rowan tree is the best preservative against evil; if a branch be woven into the roof, the house is safe for a year at least, and if mixed with the timber of a boat no storm will upset it, and no man be drowned in it for the next twelvemonth.

May Morn

As a preservative against fairy malice and darts, which at this season wound and kill, it is the custom on May morning, at sunrise, to bleed the cattle and taste of the blood mingled with milk. Men and women were also bled, and their blood was sprinkled on the ground. This practice, however, has died out, even in the remote West; but the children are still lifted through the fire when it has burned low, and the cattle are driven through the hot embers—as in ancient times both children and cattle were "passed through the fire to Moloch"—and the young men still leap through the flames after the dance round the burning bush is over, and they carry home a lighted branch of the sacred tree to give good luck to the family during the coming year.

On May morning the peasant girls delight in gathering May dew before sunrise, to beautify their faces, and they believe that the sun will then have no power over their complexions to spoil them by the summer heat; and no fire is lighted in any home until the smoke is seen rising from the chimney of the priest's house, which, to the modern world, is like the first fire on the Druid altar of old, that gave the signal of the uprising of the Sun-God.

The May-Day Dance

Dancing was the most important of the sacred rites in all ancient religions; and the circular serpent-dance round the tree has been practised from the remotest antiquity.

At the great long dance held on May Day all the people held hands and danced round a tall May bush erected on a mound, the girls wearing garlands, while the pipers and harpers, with gold and green sashes, directed the movements (in curves from right to left). The oldest worship of the world included homage to the tree and the serpent. Trees were the symbol of knowledge, and the dance round the May bush simulated the sinuous curves of the serpent.

May Eve

Great precautions must be taken on May Eve, for the fairies have fatal power over the human race upon that night, and steal the children and bewitch the cattle if they can find an opportunity; therefore no door should be left open after sunset, and young persons should not go out alone on the hills, nor listen to the singing of young girls in the night, for they are fairies in disguise, and will work harm. And, above all, fire should not be given away, for fire is the life of man; and if any food, boiled, roast, or baked, is left over from May Eve to May Day, it must not be eaten, but buried in the garden, or thrown over the boundary of the town-land for the dogs, because the fairies stole away the real food at night, and left in its place only lumps of turf sod, made to look like food, and to touch them would be fatal.

Whitsuntide

(the week that begins with Whit Sunday, or Pentecost,
which is the 50th day after Easter)

Whitsuntide has always been considered by the Irish as a very fatal and unlucky time—for the people hold that fairies and evil spirits have then great power over men and cattle, both by sea and land, and work their deadly spells with malign and mysterious efficacy. Children born at Whitsuntide, it is said, are foredoomed; they will either have the evil eye, or commit a murder, or die a violent death. Water, also, is very dangerous; no one should bathe, or go a journey where a stream has to be crossed, or sail in a boat, for the risk is great of being drowned, unless, indeed, a bride steers, and then the boat is safe from harm.

Great precautions are necessary, likewise, within the house; and no one should venture to light a candle without making the sign of the Cross over the flame to keep off evil; and young men should be very cautious not to be out late at night, for all the dead who have been drowned in the sea round about come up and ride over the waves on white horses, and hold strange revels, and try to carry off the young men, or to kill them with their fiery darts and draw them down under the sea to live with the dead for evermore.

At this season, also, the fairy queens make great efforts to carry off the fine stalwart young men of the country to the fairy palace in the cleft of the hills, or to lure them to their dancing grounds,

where they are lulled into dreams by the sweet, subtle fairy music, and forget home and kith and kindred, and never desire to return again to their own people: or even if the spell is broken, and they are brought back by some strong incantation, yet they are never the same; for everyone knows by the dream-look in their eyes that they have danced with the fairies on the hill, and been loved by one of the beautiful but fatal race, who, when they take a fancy to a handsome mortal lover, cast their spells over him with resistless power.

Hallowtide

The ancient Irish had two great divisions of the year, *Samradh* and *Geimradh*—summer and winter—corresponding to the May and November of our calendar; one represented the resurrection of nature and all things to life; the other the descent of all things to darkness and death.

La-samnah, or Hallow Eve, was considered the summer end, the first day of winter, when the Sun-God entered the kingdom of death; therefore, on that night of gloom the great sacred fire was lighted on every Druid altar to guide him on his downward path; and the Druid priests sacrificed a black sheep, and offered libations to the dead who had died within the year.

It was a weird season of dread and ill omen; and for this reason November was called by the Irish "the month of mourning." Then it was that Baal, the lord of death, summoned before him the souls of the dead to receive judgment for the works done in the human life; and on the vigil of *Saman*, or Hallow Eve, the dead had strange power over the living, and could work them harm, and take revenge for any wrong done to them while they lived. Even now, according to the popular belief, it is not safe to be near a churchyard on Hallow Eve, and people should not leave their homes after dark, or the ghosts would pursue them. For on that one night of the year power is given to the dead, and they rise from their graves and go forth amidst the living, and can work good or evil, no man hindering; and at midnight they hold a festival like the fairies of the hill, and drink red wine from fairy cups, and dance in their white shrouds to fairy music till the first red dawn of day. For Hallow Eve is the great festival of the dead, when their bonds are loosed, and they revel with mad joy in the life of the living. And if on that night you hear footsteps following you, beware of looking round; it is the dead who are behind you; and if you meet their glance, assuredly you must die.

Garland Sunday
(*The first Sunday in September*)

This was a great festival with the people from the most ancient times, and was devoted by the Irish to solemn rites in honour of their dead kindred. The garland, or hoop, was decorated the night before with coloured ribbons, but the flowers that encircled it were not plucked till the morning of the great day, and only unmarried girls were allowed to gather the flowers and wreathe the garland, for the touch of a married woman's hand in the decorations was deemed unlucky. Then all the company proceeded to the churchyard, the finest young man in the village being chosen to carry the garland. From the topmost hoop some apples were suspended by their stalks, and if one dropped off during the procession, it was considered a lucky omen for the garland-bearer, a prophecy of long life and success in love; but if an apple fell after the garland was set up in the graveyard, it was looked on as a sign of ill luck and coming evil, especially to those who were dancing at the time; for a dance always closed the festival, after prayers were said, and flowers were strewn, with weeping and wailing, over the recent graves. The Irish nature passes lightly from sorrow to mirth, and the evening that began in tears ended in feasting and dances, while the garland of hospitality was offered to the mourning strangers, who had come, perhaps, a long distance to do honour to their dead kindred.

Other Days

Presents may be given on New Year's Day, but no money should be paid away.

Never pay away money on the first Monday of the year, or you will lose your luck in gaining money all the year after.

On Twelfth night (January 6th) the people make a cake of yellow clay taken from a churchyard, then stick twelve bits of candle in it, and recite their prayers, kneeling round, until all the lights have burned down. A name is given to each light, and the first that goes out betokens death to the person whose name it bears, before the year is out.

On February 2nd, Candlemas night, the same trick is practised; twelve lighted candles are named after the family, the first whose light burns out, dies first, and so on to the last, who will be the survivor of all.

On Ash Wednesday, every one is marked on the forehead with the blessed ashes, and the black mark is retained carefully through the day, the priest himself having touched the brow with his finger. Also, a coal is brought from the priest's house to kindle the fire, for the consecrated coal brings good fortune to the house and the inmates.

If the lark sings on St. Bridget's Day (February 1) it is a good omen, and a sign of fine weather. And whoever hears it the first thing in the morning will have good luck in all he does for that whole day. St. Bridget was granted by the Lord to have every second Sunday fine so that she might preach to the converts that came to her.

Then St. Patrick greatly desired that his day should also be fine so that the people might gather together in remembrance of him, and this also was granted. So from that time forth the Saint's Day, the 17th of March, is always fine, for so it was decreed from the ancient times when he was upon earth.

On May morning the Skellig rocks go out full sail to meet the opposite rocks, which advance halfway to meet them, and then slowly retire like retreating ships.

At Midsummer (June 24) the fairies try to pass round the Baal fires in a whirlwind in order to extinguish them, but the spirits may be kept off by throwing fire at them. Then the young men are free to leap over the burning embers and to drive the cattle through the flames, while coals of fire must also be passed three times over and three times under the body of each animal.

Whitsuntide (the week beginning with Whit Sunday, which is the 50th day after Easter) is a most unlucky time; horses foaled then will grow up dangerous and kill someone.

To turn away ill-luck from a child born at that time, a grave must be dug and the infant laid in it for a few minutes. After this process the evil spell is broken, and the child is safe.

If any one takes ill at Whitsuntide there is great danger of death, for the evil spirits are on the watch to carry off victims, and no sick person should be left alone at this time, nor in the dark. Light is a great safeguard, as well as fire, against malefic influences.

In old times at Whitsuntide blood was poured out as a libation to the evil spirits; and the children and cattle were passed through two lines of fire.

Tober Maire (Mary's well), near Dundalk, has a great reputation for cures. And thousands used to visit it on Lady Day (March 25) for weak eyesight, and the lowness of heart. Nine times they must go round the well on their knees, always westward. Then drink a cup of the water, and not only are they cured of their ailment, but are as free from sin as the angels in heaven.

Foot-worship was a homage to Buddha, and it was also a Christian ceremony to wash the feet of the saints. The Irish had many superstitions about foot-water, and no woman was allowed to wash her feet in the sacred wells though the lavation was permitted to men.

If a child is fairy-struck, give it a cup of cold water in the name of Christ and make the sign of the cross over it.

Food should be left out on November Eve (Halloween) for the dead, who are then wandering about. If the food disappears, it is a sign that the spirits have taken it, for no mortal would dare to touch or eat of the food so left.

In November a distaff is placed under the head of a young man at night to make him dream of the girl he is destined to marry.

There is a singular superstition forbidding work of a certain kind to be done on St. Martin's Day, the 11th of November. No woman should spin on that day; no miller should grind his corn, and no wheel should be turned. And this custom was long held sacred, and is still observed in the Western Islands.

On St. Martin's Day when blood is spilt, whoever is signed with the blood is safe, for that year at least, from disease.

It is asserted that on Christmas morning the ass kneels down in adoration of Christ, and if a person can manage to touch the cross on the back of the animal at that particular moment the wish of his heart will be granted, whatever it may be.

An ox is still slaughtered at Christmas, though Baal is forgotten; and a lamb is sacrificed at Easter, as the Druids offered the first-lings of the flock to the Sun-God; while a goose is slain on St. Michael's Day (May 8) as a burnt-offering to the saint.

INDEX